WADDESD

BUCKINGHA

GW00632677

OPEN IN 1990

4 April–28 October. Wednesday to Sunday 1pm–5pm.

The Royal Standard of England

Free House. Known the world over
Forty Green, Beaconsfield
Buckinghamshire
Telephone: Beaconsfield 673382

We bid you welcome to our ancient hostelry. For 900 years its walls have offered shelter to the wayfarer, rich or poor alike. Charles II sought refuge here. It is known the world over; we are delighted not only to welcome those who visit us from these shores, but also the many thousands that visit us from overseas. We trust your visit will prove enjoyable and we shall have the pleasure of welcoming you many times in the future.

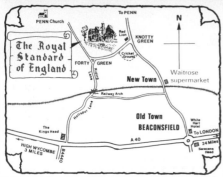

At last there is a pub that supplies good food and beer plus a wide range of wines, including some unusual ones like apricot and barley. The Royal Standard is between Beaconsfield and Forty Green. It boasts a beautiful, country atmosphere, in character with its surroundings. It is hailed to be one of the oldest public houses in the land.

The friendly greeting that awaits you on arrival will make you feel immediately at ease.

During winter come into the warmth of our coal and log fires. In summertime you can sit outside and enjoy the sun in the patio gardens. Next time you are out for a drive or want a good meal in a relaxed situation, try the Royal Standard – you won't be disappointed!

The Royal Standard of England

LET US WELCOME YOU TO THE HOME OF THE

FAMOUS
CHALFONT SHIRES

MODEL FARM

Open to the public 7 days a week. From March 1st until the
end of September. 10.00am to 4.30pm.

Mr Croft showing four of his outstanding black shires.

Some of our experienced staff at Model
Farm, left to right: Susan, Harold,
David, Michelle, Gail and Paul.
Horses: Guardsman and Fenman.

A pair of black shires being shown by
Harold Sherfield in our excellent 1910
show dray.

● *EXCELLENT TEA ROOMS* ● *SOUVENIR SHOP* ● *BLACKSMITH SHOP* ● *PICNIC AREA* ● *CHILD'S PLAY AREA* ● *PETS CORNER* ● *VINTAGE LORRIES* ● *DAILY DEMONSTRATIONS 11.30AM AND 2.30PM*

CHALFONT SHIRE CENTRE·MODEL FARM·GORELANDS
LANE·CHALFONT ST GILES HP8 4AB. TELEPHONE (02407) 2304

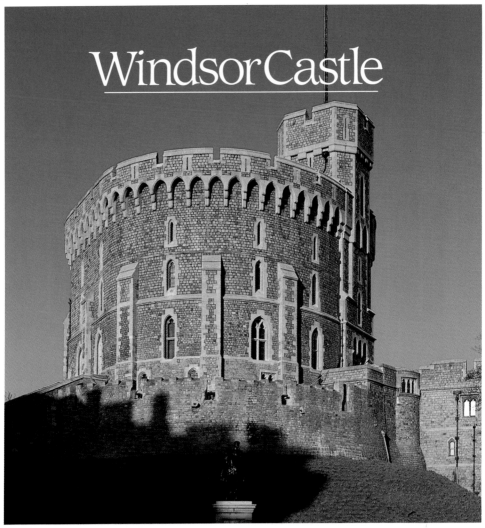

Windsor Castle

For over 900 years, Windsor Castle has served as residence and fortress for the British Monarchy, acting as a spectacular backdrop for the important Ceremonies of State, including the gatherings of The Knights of The Garter.

The State Apartments, containing many treasures from the Royal Collection, one of the finest art collections in the world, are in use on a regular basis whilst Queen Mary's Dolls' House and the Exhibition of the Queen's Presents and Royal Carriages, combine with St. George's Chapel and the architecture and the atmosphere of a place associated with the Monarchy, to provide an unrivalled insight into nine centuries of royal history.

The precincts of the castle are open free of charge. Enquiries: 0753 831118 for detailed opening arrangements

The Castle has the following areas open to the public:
- The State Apartments.
- Exhibition of The Queen's Presents and Royal Carriages.
- Queen Mary's Dolls' House.
- St George's Chapel.

Admission Charge.

Open all Year (State Apartments closed when H. M. The Queen in Official residence). Parties welcome.

How to get there:
By train – leave London Waterloo Station every 30 mins Monday to Saturday and every hour on Sunday. Telephone 01-928 5100 for details.
By coach – leave Victoria Coach Station every 30 mins. Telephone 01-668 7261 for details

Spend the day in the Dark Continent.
(Some of our employees hope you'll never leave.)

A hundred yards north of our gates and you're in the African bush.

You'll see Rhino, Zebra, Giraffe and Eland. (The largest of all the antelopes.)

But always remember, this is Lion Country, home to Britain's biggest pride of lions.

In fact Windsor's got more big game than any other safari park. (At our Sea World show you'll meet Britain's only Killer Whale.)

We'll even take you by boat into the deepest, darkest jungle in the whole of deepest, darkest Berkshire.

Directions to our address are given below. Our employees would just love you to drop in on them.

M4 Junction 6, M25 Junction 13, M3 Junction 3.

Windsor Safari Park, Winkfield Road, Windsor, Berks. SL4 4AY

Tel: 0753 869841.

Open every day except Christmas Day.

WINDSOR SAFARI PARK

The African Adventure

8

WOBURN WILD ANIMAL KINGDOM SAFARI PARK

Open Daily   Mid March to October
Telephone   Woburn (0525) 290407

The management reserve the right to vary:- the times of opening and closing, the animals on display, the admission price, and also the availability of any attraction or facility, without notice.

Blenheim Palace

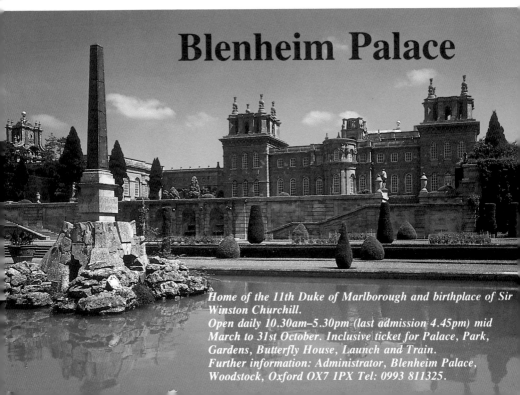

Home of the 11th Duke of Marlborough and birthplace of Sir Winston Churchill.
Open daily 10.30am–5.30pm (last admission 4.45pm) mid March to 31st October. Inclusive ticket for Palace, Park, Gardens, Butterfly House, Launch and Train.
Further information: Administrator, Blenheim Palace, Woodstock, Oxford OX7 1PX Tel: 0993 811325.

Warwick Castle
The finest mediaeval castle in England

Open every day
(Except Christmas day)
Telephone: Warwick 495421 (Daytime only)

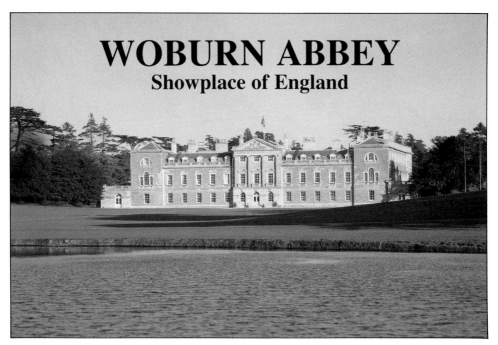

WOBURN ABBEY
Showplace of England

OPEN: SATS/SUNS 1 JAN–1 APRIL AND EVERY DAY 2 APRIL–28 OCT
Woburn Abbey, Woburn, Bedfordshire MK43 0TP. Telephone: Woburn (0525) 290666

BEKONSCOT

The oldest model village in the world invites you to lose yourself in a wonderland of miniature

OPEN SEVEN DAYS A WEEK
1st MARCH TO 31st OCT.
10am to 5pm
Can you believe our entrance prices?
£1.80 Adults. 90 pence Children

* PARADISE FOR THE
  PHOTOGRAPHER
* WONDERLAND FOR THE
  MODEL ENTHUSIAST
* HEAVEN FOR THE GARDENER
* A *MUST* FOR THE CHILDREN
* IN FACT A TREAT FOR THE
  WHOLE FAMILY.

BEKONSCOT MODEL VILLAGE
WARWICK ROAD · BEACONSFIELD
BUCKS · HP9 2PL
TELEPHONE: (0494) 672919

CORAL REEF
BRACKNELL'S WATER WORLD

CORAL POOLS
A treasure chest of adventures for all ages and all levels. Attractions include:
- Little Corals Toddlers Pools
- Pirate Ship with Water Cannons
- Snake River Flumes
- Emerald Forest Rain Cloud
- Wild Water Rapids
- and many many more

SAUNA WORLD
Toe to toe relaxation. The ultimate body experience in an atmosphere of soft music and tropical warmth.
- Scented Saunas
- Japanese Steam Room
- Sunny Gym's • Sunbeds
- Cool Pool • Sunken Footspa

COCONUT GROVE
After you've dodged the Water Cannons, explored the Pirate Ship, ridden the Rapids, why not whet your appetite with a refreshing drink in the bar. Exotic cocktails, soft drinks, or a refreshing cup of tea are all available. Or visit the Restaurant for the finest fare from snacks to beautifully cooked meals.

The Riches Of The Reef Are Waiting . . .
Bracknell's new Water World is water at its most glorious. Inspired by the most wonderful water experiences from around the world, the lure of the reef is irresistible. Come and discover its riches for yourself.

- Ample FREE car parking
- Access and Visa accepted
- Easy to reach:
  M3 Junction 3 – 3.7 miles
  M4 Junction 10 – 4.1 miles
- For details of opening times:
  Telephone: (0344) 862525
  (0344) 862484
  (24 hour information service)

Coral Reef, Bracknell's Water World, Nine Mile Ride, Bracknell, Berkshire RG12 4JQ. Telephone: (0344) 862525
(0344) 862484 (24 hour information service)

BRACKNELL FOREST BOROUGH COUNCIL

KNEBWORTH·HOUSE
HERTFORDSHIRE

HISTORIC HOME OF THE LYTTON FAMILY SINCE 1490

the Lytton Family
1490·1990
500
years
Knebworth House

For details see Hertfordshire section

14

WHERE TO GO

THAMES & CHILTERNS

CONTENTS

LEGEND TO MAPS

M4	Motorway		National Parks and Areas of Outstanding Natural Beauty
	Primary Route	– – – –	Long Distance Footpath
	Other A Road		Railway
	B Road	✈	Airport
	Minor Road	i	Tourist Information Centre

Castle	Boating Activity	Botanical Garden	Theatre
House of Interest	Bridge of Interest	Vineyard	Craft Centre
Opening Restricted	Holiday Boat & Cruiser Hire	Industrial Interest	Garden Centre
Garden	Monument	Agricultural Interest	Horse Racing
House and Garden	Zoo	Archaeological Site	Motor Racing
Church of Interest	Wildlife Park	Battle Site	Aerial Activity
Cathedral	Bird Sanctuary	Other Places of Interest	Football League Ground
Abbey	Nature Trail	Water Skiing	Windmill
Museum	Picnic Site	Swimming Pool	Caravan Site
Literary Landmark	Country Park	Recreation Centre	Camping Site
Ancient Monument			Narrow Gauge Railway

Scale

0 1 2 3 4 5 —————— 10 Miles

Based upon the ORDNANCE SURVEY maps with the sanction
of the controller of HM Stationery Office. Crown copyright reserved

Cartography prepared by
ESTATE PUBLICATIONS

The Thames & Chilterns

The five counties of the Thames and Chilterns Region fan out in a wide arc to the west and north of London, making them easily accessible by air, motorway and rail. It is the contrasts, not the distances that are great; and this area, crossed by famous hills and rivers, distils the essence of England. However long your stay, you will not exhaust the pleasures it has to offer; from the homely comforts of a thatched cottage to the sophisticated charm of a palatial country hotel; from the welcoming pleasures of a cosy pub to the gracious elegance of fine dining; from the peace of an ancient village church to the breathtaking splendour of a soaring medieval cathedral.

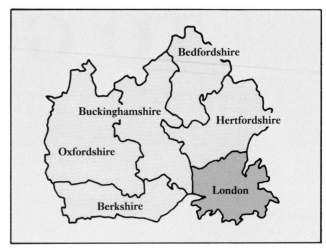

Crossing the region and passing many of its most famous sights, the Royal River Thames flows beneath the walls of Windsor Castle, the home of English monarchs since the time of William the Conqueror. Upstream it drifts through countryside that could only be in England, past pretty towns and villages like Henley,

The Chiltern Hills

Cookham and Marlow.

1990 marks the centenary of another famous waterway. The beautifully restored 87-mile Kennet and Avon Canal will reopen, once again linking the River Thames at Reading in Berkshire with Bristol. This triumph is the result of many years of dedication and effort, and restores the canal's prominent place in English navigation.

To the north, Oxfordshire eludes brief description. Its fertile fields cover the hills like a patchwork of greens and browns, stitched together with seams of dry-stone wall and hedgerow. Oxford, on the other hand, hums with the excitement of one of the world's great universities. At its heart, hundreds of architectural and cultural treasures blend easily (though it was not always so) with a modern commercial centre.

But there is no monopoly on history, and in nearby Hertfordshire, St Albans was already an important European centre in Roman times. Subsequently a fine abbey was established there in memory of England's first Christian martyr and still later, Hatfield House was the childhood home of Queen Elizabeth I.

The lower part of neighbouring Buckinghamshire is crossed diagonally by the wide sweep of the beautiful, beech-covered Chiltern Hills. The Vale of Aylesbury is studded with impressive historic houses, such as the Rothschild's fabled Waddesdon Manor, Hughenden Manor (home of Benjamin Disraeli) and Claydon House. In the north of the county is England's newest city, the much-debated Milton Keynes, a model of planned development and home of the innovative Open University.

Bedfordshire in the north typifies the region's diversity of landscape and interests. Its southern end catches the tip of the Chilterns and is the home of Luton International Airport. Although it has many major arteries linking London and points

The Royal River Thames

north, much of the county's charm lies with its expanses of peaceful, rural landscape. John Bunyan, the author of the renowned *The Pilgrim's Progress*, spent most of his life in and around the town of Bedford.

So whether you seek rural tranquility, the perfect country church, historic associations or beautiful waterways, the Thames and Chilterns is sure to satisfy. We welcome you!

Using Where to Go

For ease, the attractions are listed alphabetically by county and nearest town heading. The numbers following each entry are keyed to the map at the beginning of each county, and the letters E.H. or N.T. following a name indicate that the property is managed by English Heritage or the National Trust, respectively. Please note that because most waterways cross county boundaries, the boating firms are listed alphabetically by waterway in the section entitled "Leisure Afloat".

17

Dunstable Priory

Bedfordshire

Bedfordshire is a county of great natural beauty, from the high point of the Dunstable Downs in the south to the River Great Ouse winding its way gently through the north. It is a beauty that is very accessible to visitors, as many country parks, nature reserves, riverside walks and grand estates are open to the public. Many of the open spaces are under the care of North Bedfordshire Borough Council and Bedfordshire County Council which have provided extra amenities for visitors.

The area has many historic connections — prehistoric man, the Saxons, Romans and Normans have all left their mark. The 4,000-year-old Icknield Way and Roman Watling Street both cross the county.

Bedfordshire's most famous son is probably John Bunyan, the 17th-C. Nonconformist preacher and author. He was born at Harrowden and was imprisoned for his beliefs for many years in Bedford County Gaol.

Among the many stately homes to visit in the county are two of England's finest – Woburn Abbey and Luton Hoo. Woburn is also the home of the famous Wild Animal Kingdom and Safari Park, and the Wild Animal Park at Whipsnade is well known for its breeding of endangered species.

Thatched cottage, South Beds

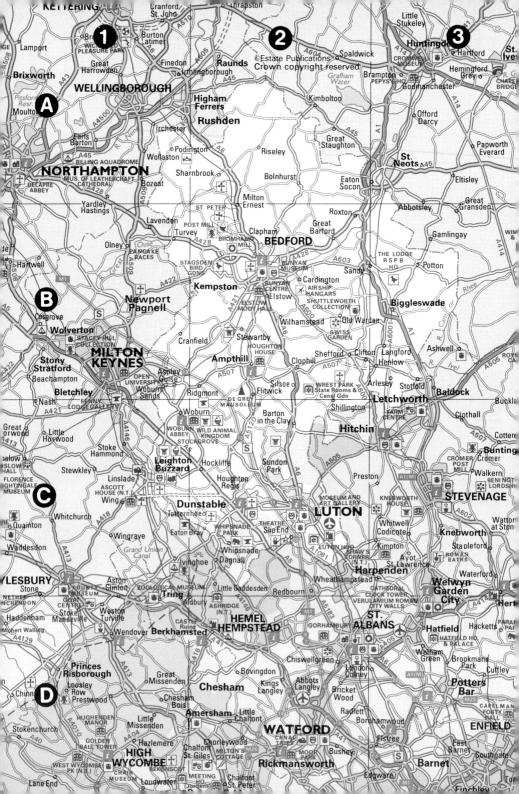

Bedford

The Great Ouse, one of England's most attractive rivers, flows through the county town of Bedford, a long-established centre of education. The Borough Council has greatly enhanced this stretch of the river by creating miles of riverside walks and gardens, restoring locks and constructing a marina. Bedford's treatment of its riverside is exemplary and even includes, along the Embankment, a special fragrance garden for the blind. The river plays host to an annual regatta the second Saturday in July, and a colourful river festival featuring floats and fireworks is held the weekend of Spring Bank Holiday in even-numbered years.

The life of Separatist preacher and writer John Bunyan centred around Bedford, and today a statue on St Peter's Green and the Bunyan Museum mark his place as a pioneer of religious liberty and freedom of conscience. A 'John Bunyan Trail' leaflet showing places associated with his life is available from the Tourist Information Centre.

Bedford Museum 2B

Open: *Tue–Sat 11–5, Sun, B.H. Mon 2–5. Closed Good Fri and 23–26 Dec. Tel: Bedford (0234) 53323.*
Recently rehoused in a tastefully restored brewery, the museum's collection covers local archaeology, history, domestic and agricultural bygones and the area's lace-making tradition. Visiting exhibitions are also regularly featured.

Bromham Mill 2B

Open: *Apr–Oct, Wed, Thur, Fri 10.30–4.30; Sat, Sun, B.H. Mon 11–6.*
A picnic site has been developed on the banks of the Ouse at Bromham Mill, three miles west of Bedford, just north of the A 428. The restored 17th-C. buildings now house a museum of milling, a natural history room and exhibitions of work by local artists.

Bunyan Meeting Free Church and Bunyan Museum 2B

Open: *Apr–Sept, Tue–Sat 2–4. Tel: Bedford (0234) 58870.*
The life and work of Free Church advocate John Bunyan (1638–1688) are explored at 55 Mill Street. Following the Restoration of Charles II, Bunyan (then 32) was imprisoned for his dissenting beliefs, along with 60 others, and spent the next 12 years in the Bedford County Gaol. During this period he wrote numerous tracts and his major allegory, *The Pilgrim's Progress*. The museum houses a large collection of translations of this work, as well as personal effects and memorabilia. See also Elstow Moot Hall.

Cardington 2B

South-east of Bedford is Cardington Lock, where you'll find the country's first artificial slalom course for canoes. At Cardington itself are two gigantic hangers, large enough to house an ocean liner and visible for miles around. One of these is now the headquarters of the revived British airship industry. It was from these hangers in 1930 that the ill-fated airship R101 set off on its journey to India.

John Bunyan's statue, Bedford

21

Cecil Higgins Art Gallery 2B

Open: *Tue–Fri 12.30–5, Sat 11–5, Sun 2–5, B.H. Mon 12.30–5. Closed Good Fri, Christmas and Boxing Day. Tel: Bedford (0234) 211222.*

Near the riverside gardens in Castle Close, and on the site of the old Bedford Castle, is the internationally known Cecil Higgins Art Gallery, part of which is set out as a re-created Victorian mansion. Here there are outstanding collections of English water-colours, drawings, prints, procelain, glass, miniatures, textiles, lace and silver.

Elstow Moot Hall 2B

Open: *Easter–Oct, Tue–Sat, B.H. Mon 2–5, Sun 2–5.30. Tel: Bedford (0234) 668899.*

John Bunyan was born in 1638 in the hamlet of Harrowden on the edge of Elstow, one mile south of Bedford. His early (and somewhat irresolute) life was spent here, and visitors can see the abbey where he was baptized, rang the bells and worshipped. Beside it are the village green where he played as a child and the 15th-C. Moot Hall where there are exhibits about his life.

Elstow Moot Hall

Houghton House (E.H.) 2B

Open: *any reasonable time.*

There are other local Bunyan connections. A bit farther south, just outside **Ampthill** on the A418 is a steep hill thought to be Bunyan's 'Hill of Difficulty' and nearby stand the ruins of Houghton House, a 17th-C. building said to be his 'House Beautiful'.

Stagsden Bird Gardens 2B

Open: *daily 11–6 or dusk. Tel: Oakley (02302) 2745.*

Five miles west of Bedford on the A422, Stagsden is a breeding centre for over 200 species of birds, including owls, cranes, pheasants, waterfowl, poultry and birds of prey. There is also a rose garden.

Stevington Windmill 2B

Open: *daily 10–7 or dusk. Keys from The Royal George Inn, Silver Street, Stevington, on payment of small returnable deposit. Keys not issued to minors. Tel: Oakley (02302) 2184.*

The Stevington Post Mill, about 5 miles north-west of Bedford, was built between 1765 and 1770.

Both it and the nearby Bromham Watermill are in the care of the Bedfordshire County Council.

Dunstable

Set on the crossroads of the ancient Icknield Way and Roman Watling Street, Dunstable has been inhabited by man for thousands of years.

High on the summit of **Dunstable Downs** are five Bronze Age burial mounds known locally as The Five Knolls. The Downs form a beautiful natural feature and give commanding views. Bedfordshire County Council has provided an Interpretation Centre and picnic area – the perfect viewpoint for watching the activities of the London Gliding Club.

The nearby village of **Totternhoe** is dwarfed by the Totternhoe Knolls with a motte and bailey at the highest point. The Knolls are kept as a nature reserve and managed by the Naturalists' Trust and Bedfordshire County Council; there are nature trails and a picnic site.

Whipsnade Wild Animal Park 2C

Open: *Mon–Sat 10–6 or dusk; Sun, B.H. Mon 10–7 or dusk. Tel: Whipsnade (0582) 872171.*

Set in 600 acres of beautiful parkland, Whipsnade Wild Animal Park is home to over 2,800 animals, many in large, open paddocks. Whipsnade is the country's largest conservation centre specialising in the breeding of rare and endangered animals, such as cheetahs, Prezewalski's horses and Indian rhinos.

It also has family favourites such as chimps, bears, zebras, penguins, tigers and many others. Throughout the season there are free sea-lion shows with underwater viewing, working elephant demonstrations, birds-of-prey flying shows, 'Animal Encounters' and 'Meet the Animals' sessions with a keeper to accompany you.

The sea-lions at Whipsnade Wild Animal Park

Leighton Buzzard

Already a thriving market town at the time of *Domesday Book*, Leighton Buzzard in modern times has become famous for sand – even exporting it to the Sahara Desert! It retains its market-town character with many 17th- and 18th-C. buildings still standing in the High Street.

The 15th-C. pentagonal market-cross at the centre of town has witnessed many contrasting scenes, from witch trials and horse auctions to the calling of marriage banns. The Cenotaph, in Church Square, is thought to be the largest single block of granite quarried in the British Isles. It is 25 feet high and weighs 22 tons.

Leighton Buzzard Theatre and Arts Centre 1C

Tel: Leighton Buzzard (0525) 378310

Nearby in Lake Street stands the modern Theatre and Arts Centre which offers a variety of entertainment by visiting professional artists and theatre companies.

Leighton Buzzard Railway

Leighton Buzzard Railway 1C

Open: *Apr–7 Oct, Sun; 21 July– 29 Aug, Sat, Wed. Also Good Fri, B.H. Mon, Easter Sat. Trains at intervals between 11 and 4.30 (last train at 3 on Sat and Wed.) Special school trains by appointment 2–6 July. Also special events throughout season. Tel: Leighton Buzzard (0525) 373888.*

At Page's Park, visitors can enjoy the delights of the Leighton Buzzard Railway. Now extensively rebuilt and restocked with locomotives from all over the world, this two-foot-gauge railway was built in 1919 to carry sand from the quarries north of town. The little line wends its way for 5½ miles from the terminus into open countryside and back.

Stockgrove Country Park 1C

Tel: Leighton Buzzard (0525) 237760.

Between Leighton Buzzard and Woburn is Stockgrove Country Park, which has a stream, an ornamental lake and picnic facilities in its 74 acres of woodland and park. A visitors' centre has recently opened.

Across the River Ouzel from Leighton Buzzard is **Linslade**. The District Council has created a riverside walk beside the Ouzel and the Grand Union Canal, linking Old Linslade and Linslade.

23

Luton

The fortunes of Luton – the largest town in Bedfordshire – were largely founded on the straw-hat industry. Today it is known mainly for its car industry, airport, and modern city-centre shopping precinct. There are open spaces too, with no fewer than seven parks, totalling 475 acres, in the town.

Luton Hoo 2C

Open: *12 Apr–14 Oct daily except Mon (open B.H. Mon). House and Collection: 1.30–5.45; Gardens and Park: 12–6. Last entry at 5. Tel: Luton (0582) 22955.*

South of Luton is Luton Hoo, home of the Wernher family since 1900. Set in parkland laid out by 'Capability' Brown, the house was originally built by Robert Adam in 1767. However, it is for the matchless Wernher Collection that it is probably most famous. This is a treasure house of Old Masters, magnificent tapestries and furniture, medieval ivories, Renaissance jewellery and procelain. Perhaps most noteworthy of all is the unique collection of Russian Fabergé jewellery and portraits and mementoes of the Russian Imperial family. These were inherited by the late Lady Zia Wernher, daughter of the Grand Duke Michael Mikhailovitch and grandmother of the present owner of Luton Hoo, Nicholas Phillips.

Luton International Airport 2C

Tel: Luton (0582) 405100.

Luton International Airport, south-east of the town, has expanded greatly since its modest beginnings in 1938. It is now Britain's third-largest airport in terms of international charter flights and still growing. The ever-improving range of facilities and the number of flights available to passengers have established Luton's airport as an alternative London gateway.

A new Tourist Information Centre has recently opened in the main terminal.

Luton Musuem and Art Gallery 2C

Open: *Mon–Sat 10–5, Sun 1–5, Tel: Luton (0582) 36941.*

Outside the town centre the Luton Museum and Art Gallery occupies a Victorian mansion in Wardown Park.

There are several exhibitions of local interest, including the Luton Life Gallery, archaeology and natural history displays, and in the Children's Gallery, a display of toys, dolls and games. A continuous programme of events is held, including two annual art exhibitions.

Stockwood Craft Museum and Gardens 2C

Open: *Apr–28 Oct, Wed–Sat 10–5, Sun 10–6. Tel: Luton (0582) 38714.*

Stockwood Craft Museum and

Luton Hoo

The Shuttleworth Collection, Old Warden

Gardens lies south of Luton off Farley Hill in the grounds of Stockwood Park. Housed in an 18th-C. stable block, the exhibits feature a wide range of local trades and crafts, including a reconstructed thatched cottage and a working reconstruction of an old forge. Craft workshops also help bring the past alive. A series of period gardens is in the process of development. Refreshments are available at the weekends in the greenhouse tearoom.

Sundon Hills Country Park 2C

The 96 acres of the Sundon Hills Country Park north of Luton form part of the Bedfordshire Chilterns Area of Outstanding Natural Beauty. Here the landscape varies between steep scrub-covered slopes, open chalk meadowland and wooded areas. The Country Park offers many outstanding views across miles of peaceful and inviting countryside.

Woodside Farm and Wild Fowl Park 2C

Open: *Mon–Sat 8–5. Closed Christmas and Boxing Day and New Year's Day. Tel: Luton (0582) 841044.*
In seven acres of quiet countryside off Mancroft Road near Slip End south of Luton, Woodside offers something for all the family. The wildfowl park contains a large collection of rare and pure-breed fowl. Children can mingle with the animals, feed their favourite pets and enjoy the Tarzan Trail, Fort and Nurseryland. The traditional farm shop offers fresh farm produce, goat and sheep products and a 'pick-your-own' free-range egg unit. 'Fieldfare' arts and crafts centre displays a wide selection of hand-made gifts for country lovers. Coffee shop and large car park.

Old Warden (nr Biggleswade)
The Shuttleworth Collection 2B

Open: *daily, Nov–Mar 10–4; Apr–Oct 10–5. Last admission one hour before closing. Closed week of Christmas and New Year. Tel: Biggleswade (0767 27) 288.*
Aviation and automotive history are featured in the pretty estate village of Old Warden. The Shuttleworth Collection of Historic Aeroplanes and Road Vehicles gives visitors the chance to see some of the world's earliest and most famous aircraft in the air. The collection was founded more than 50 years ago by Richard Shuttleworth to ensure that examples of great engineering achievements did not disappear. Flying displays are generally held on the first Sunday of the month, May to October. Picnic area, restaurant and cafeteria.

Wrest Park Gardens, Silsoe

The Swiss Garden 2B

Open: *Easter–Oct, Wed–Sun, B.H. Mon 1.30–6 (last admission 5.15).*
The unique Swiss Garden was developed in the early 1800s as an extension to the gardens of Old Warden Park and takes its name from the tiny thatched Swiss Cottage in the centre. The garden sadly fell into disrepair in the post-war years, but has been carefully restored by the Bedfordshire County Council. It features numerous trees and plants, some rare. Adjacent lakeside picnic site.

Podington

Podington Garden Centre 1A

Open: *daily 9–5.30 (phone for late-night summer openings). Tel: Rushden (0933) 53656.*
On the High Street in a delightful village in the North Bedfordshire countryside you'll find Podington Garden Centre, established in

1977 by Colin and Norma Read. All year round there are thousands of plants to browse among, both indoors in spacious covered areas

Bedfordshire Farm and Country Holiday Group

For North Bedfordshire, Tel: Bedford (0234) 870234; for South Bedfordshire, Tel: Flitwick (0525) 712316.
To enjoy the splendid Bedfordshire countryside thoroughly, try some real country living in buildings ranging from 16th-C. thatched cottages to rambling Edwardian houses. Traditional farmhouse accommodation is offered by the members of the Bedfordshire Farm and Country Holiday Group, with prices from £12 per person per night for bed and breakfast, or from £70 per week self-catering.

and outside in attractive display gardens. There's also a coffee shop.

Santa Pod Raceway 1A

Tel: Rushden (0933) 313250.
Santa Pod, the home of European Drag Racing, is the only purpose-built drag strip in this country. As well as drag-race meetings from March to November, the raceway, located at the Podington Airfield, is also used for special exhibitions and outdoor demonstrations.

Sandy

The Lodge Reserve 3B

Open: *Mon–Fri 9–5; Sat, Sun 10–5 (12–4.30 Christmas–Easter). Tel: Sandy (0767) 80551.*
The Lodge Reserve at Sandy, east of Bedford, is the headquarters of the Royal Society for the Protection of Birds. More than 140 species of birds have been recorded in the reserve, which is set around a magnificent Tudor-style house built in 1870.

26

Silsoe

Wrest Park (E.H.) 2B

Open: *13 Apr–30 Sept, Sat, Sun, B.H. Mon 10–6. Tel: Silsoe (0525) 60152.*

East of the village of Silsoe are the extensive 18th- and 19th-C. gardens of Wrest Park. The finest is, perhaps, the Great Garden, laid out between 1706 and 1740 by the Duke of Kent. Other features include the Painted Pavilion, Chinese bridge, lake and classical temple. Some staterooms of the house, largely rebuilt in the French baroque style in the 1830s, are also on show. Cafeteria in the Orangery.

Woburn

Woburn Abbey 2C

Open: *Jan–Apr, Sat, Sun; Park: 10.30–3.45; Abbey: 11–4 (last entry). 2 Apr–28 Oct, daily; Park: 10–4.45; Abbey: Mon–Sat 11–5 (last entry); Sun, B.H. Mon 11–5.30 (last entry). Tel: Woburn (0525) 290666.*

Woburn Abbey, north-east of Leighton Buzzard is one of the finest showplaces in England. It has been the home of the Dukes of Bedford for more than 300 years and is set in a magnificent 3,000-acre deer park. The house was rebuilt in the mid-18th C. and extensively altered later that century by Henry Holland, the Prince Regent's architect. The Abbey contains an important and extensive art collection, including paintings by Canaletto, Rembrandt, Holbein, Velázques and many others.

Tennis Coaching International 2A

Tel: Oakley (02302) 2914.
One of Britain's original and best tennis coaching centres is to be found at Woodlands, Milton Ernest, north of Bedford. From a beautiful 17th-C. listed house, Tennis Coaching International runs residential and non-residential courses.

Woburn Wild Animal Kingdom Safari Park 2C

Open: *Mid-Mar–Oct, daily 10–5. Tel: Woburn (0525) 290246.*
Woburn Wild Animal Kingdom is Britain's largest drive-through safari park. It has magnificent tigers, lions, rhinos, hippos, giraffes, monkeys, camels, Canadian timber wolves and many other species to admire. There are working elephant displays, sea-lion and parrot shows and a pets corner. All the attractions are included in one admission charge.

The Chinese Dairy, Woburn Abbey

The Savill Garden, Windsor

Berkshire

Royal Berkshire is one of the smallest of the English shire counties, but certainly one of the most beautiful and most varied.

It stretches from the outskirts of London westward to the border with Wiltshire and includes the bustling towns of Windsor and Maidenhead and Bracknell, as well as peaceful stretches of unspoilt countryside in the west. The River Thames defines half of its northern boundary, and in the south the Kennet and Avon Canal is being extensively restored into a peaceful cruiseway which eventually will link the Thames to Bath once again.

The county town of Reading received its charter in 1253 and was once the home of a powerful Benedictine monastery. Today it is a successful mix of old and new, with parks and gardens, the canal and abbey ruins, happily combined with a fine modern shopping area.

To the west lie the attractive market towns of Newbury and Hungerford in the Kennet Valley. Newbury is celebrated for its racecourse and Spring Festival; Hungerford for its serene setting on the Kennet and Avon Canal and unusual antiques arcade. Both towns saw fierce battles during the Civil War.

There are historic houses for your pleasure – places like Basildon Park and Stratfield Saye, and, of course, there is Windsor, home of Her Majesty the Queen, visited by so many every year.

Here you can enjoy the Castle and rich pageantry, or simply enjoy a walk in magnificent surroundings.

Donnington Castle, near Newbury

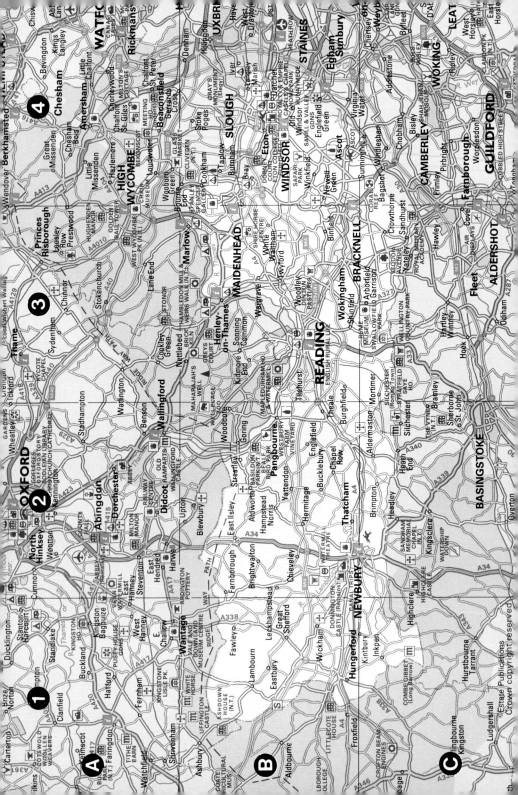

Ascot

Ascot Racecourse 4B

For details of meetings, send s.a.e. to The Racing Information Bureau, Winkfield Road, Ascot, Berks SL5 7HX. Tel: Ascot (0990) 25912.

Ascot has one of the most famous racecourses in the world. The first race meeting was held there more than 270 years ago, when Queen Anne drove from Windsor Castle with her courtiers to attend a day's sport on Ascot Common. The year was 1711 and horse-racing then was a sport of little consequence. Today, the meetings at Ascot provide occasions for great elegance and pageantry. The highlight of Ascot's year is undoubtedly the Royal Meeting in June, when each afternoon the Queen and other members of the Royal Family process round the course in five open landaus before the racing begins.

In north Ascot, quite close to the racecourse, is a special place to sample the best of British cooking, including Crown Estate venison. **The Ascot Guinea** is the 'sister' of the famous Guinea Restaurant near London's Berkeley Square (see Eating and Drinking).

Ascot Vineyard 4B

Open: daily 12–dusk. Tel: Ascot (0344) 23563.

This part of Berkshire is a wine-producing area. Ascot Vineyard on Winkfield Road was laid down in 1979, the first vineyard established on the Crown Lands since the reign of Henry II. Since then it has been enlarged and has won national awards. Visitors are warmly welcomed and group tours, lectures and wine-tasting can be organized by prior appointment.

Austin Desmond Fine Art 4B

Open: Mon–Sat 10–5.30. 3 High Street, Sunninghill, Berks. Tel: Ascot (0990) 291201.

A fine-art gallery near Ascot featuring regular exhibitions of work by modern British and contemporary artists.

Bracknell

Conceived in 1949 as one of nine 'New Towns' outside London, Bracknell's planned development has resulted in a thriving and balanced community of 50,000. Now a major business and commercial centre, it enjoys a traffic-free shopping area and numerous cultural and entertainment facilities.

Coral Reef 4C

Open: daily. Tel: Bracknell (0344) 862494.

Fittingly billed as 'Bracknell's Water World', this brand new facility at the junction of Nine Mile Ride and the Bagshot Road boasts a leisure pool with three flumes, rapids, a 'Pirate Ship', volcano and rain clouds! The Sauna World includes saunas, steam rooms and a cool pool.

John Nike Leisuresport Complex 3B

Open: daily. Tel: Bracknell (0344) 860033.

This major sports centre on John Nike Way features an ice rink, artificial ski slope, health suite, snooker club, sports shop and restaurant.

South Hill Park Arts Centre and Wilde Theatre 3B

Open: daily. Tel: Bracknell (0344) 427272.

At Birch Hill, just off the A322 Bagshot Road, this attractive arts complex in 16 acres of parkland offers an exceptional range of theatre, dance, cinema, sculpture, exhibitions and music.

Cookham

The popular Thames-side village of Cookham is one of the places where the colourful ceremony of swan-upping takes place. In the third week of July, the Royal Swan Keeper catches all the new cygnets and decides their ownership.

The Thames at Cookham

Hungerford

A quiet market town near the River Kennet and the canal, Hungerford has much to interest the visitor. Its historic past is reflected in many lovely buildings, particularly those lining the wide High Street. Visitors will be delighted by its unusual antiques arcade. The town is also proud of its Hocktide Ceremony. Visit on the second Tuesday after Easter and you will see the ancient Court Leet meeting to elect officers. Two Tutti-men and the Orange Scrambler visit every house in the High Street with commoners rights and demand a penny from the men and a kiss from the women.

Courage Shire Horse Centre

Littlecote House 1B

Open: *Apr–Sept daily 10–6. Tel: Hungerford (0488) 84000.*
Two miles west of Hungerford, this magnificent Tudor estate has been transformed into an exciting, award-winning attraction where visitors can see history come to life.

The mansion houses a unique collection of Cromwellian armour and in the grounds there are daily displays of jousting and falconry, a re-created 17th-C. village, a rare-breeds farm, a cleverly designed adventure playground, a little steam railway and an excavated Roman villa. Special events are also organized throughout the year.

Inglewood Health Hydro 1B

Tel: Hungerford (0488) 82022.
At Kintbury, west of Newbury in the serene setting of a stately home, is Inglewood Health Hydro, a residential centre for weight reduction, stress relief and fitness. Set in 50 acres of parkland, it is a haven from the noise and strain of the outside world.

Maidenhead

In Edwardian days, Maidenhead was the scene for many a champagne and punting party. Today it has developed into a popular residential town with good road and rail connections and a pedestrianized shopping area. A beautiful balustraded bridge built in 1772 by Sir Robert Taylor takes the A4 road across the Thames. Brunel's Great Western Railway bridge of 1838 was remarkable in its day as the widest span ever achieved with bricks.

Courage Shire Horse Centre 3B

Open: *Mar–Oct daily 11–5 (last admission 4). Tel: Littlewick Green (0628) 824848.*
Just outside Maidenhead on the A4 at Maidenhead Thicket near Littlewick Green, the brewing firm Courage has established its Shire Horse Centre. Up to twelve of these gentle giants can be seen here, each standing over 18 hands high and weighing about a ton.

This is a working stable where visitors will often see a farrier, wheelwright or cooper at work or be lucky enough to watch a horse being plaited, groomed and harnessed before an appearance. Brilliantly polished sets of harness and brass are displayed together with hundreds of rosettes and trophies won by these noble animals. Free guided tours run throughout the day and there's also an audio-visual presentation, a tearoom and a sourvenir shop.

Newbury

The busy and historic town of Newbury grew up to serve the surrounding farmland and stands at the crossroads of the main routes from London to the west and from Southampton to the Midlands. These routes were of great strategic importance during the Civil War in the mid-17th C. when Cavaliers twice clashed with Roundheads near the town.

Today the town is internationally known for its racecourse and Spring Festival. There are also pleasant towpath walks. Motor-barge canal trips leave Newbury Wharf, and horse-drawn canal trips leave from Kintbury Lock throughout the summer (see Leisure Afloat).

Newbury Spring Festival

Open: *8–19 May. For details of events– music, drama and the arts Tel: Newbury (0635) 32421.*

Donnington Castle 2B

Open: *any reasonable time.*
High on a hill overlooking the
village of Donnington, just north
of Newbury, stand the ruins of
Donnington Castle, beseiged and
largely destroyed in the Civil War.
Only the 14th-C. gatehouse (still
imposing) and the Civil War
earthworks remain.

Highclere Castle 2C

Open: *Jul–Sept, Wed–Sun and
Aug B.H. Mon 2–6. Tel: Highclere
(0635) 253210.*
Four and one-half miles south of
Newbury, Highclere Castle is the
seat of the Earl and Countess of
Carnarvon. It is renowned for its
priceless display of Egyptian
treasures, some only recently
rediscovered after lying hidden
behind concealed panels in the
castle for many years. It was the
fifth Earl, a celebrated
archaeologist, who with Howard
Carter discovered them and the
tomb of Tutankhamen. A room in
the Castle records his
explorations. Other rooms in this
grand Victorian building, built in
1938 by Sir Charles Barry,
architect of the Houses of
Parliament, form an apt setting for
the family's collections of
furnishings, carving, portraits and
Old Masters. There are walled
and secret gardens, yew walks,
porticos and tropical
conservatories. The landscaped
parkland surrounding the castle
was partly designed by 'Capability'
Brown. Country teas are served
and there is a Castle Garden
Centre.

Newbury District Museum 2B

Open: *Apr–Sept, Mon, Tue,
Thur–Sat 10–6; Sun, B.H. Mon
2–6. Oct–Mar, Mon, Tue, Thur–
Sat 10–4. Tel: Newbury (0635)
30511.*
The museum occupies a 17th-C.
Wool Hall and 18th-C. Granary at
The Wharf buildings, near the
town centre. Its collections
emphasize local archaeology,
natural history, costume,

Highclere Castle

traditional crafts, ballooning, the
canal and the local impact of the
Civil War.

Watermill Theatre 2B

Tel: Newbury (0635) 46044.
Near Donnington in the tiny
hamlet of Bagnor is the unique
Watermill Theatre on the banks of
the River Lambourn. Here
professional theatre is presented in
the perfect setting of a 19th-C.
watermill that once produced
high-quality writing paper.
Performances take place from late
March through the Christmas
holidays. Licensed restaurant;
picnics not permitted.

Call **The Bee Line**
for local bus services
throughout Berkshire and
South Buckinghamshire,
coach links from Heathrow to
Reading and Londonlink
coach services from London to
Berkshire, as well as tours,
excursions and private
charters.
*Tel: Newbury (0635) 40743;
Reading (0734) 581358;
Bracknell (0344) 424938;
Maidenhead (0628) 21344;
High Wycombe (0494)
20941.*

Pangbourne

Pangbourne is a delightful Thames-side town with an attractive lock, weir and toll bridge. Local associations with Kenneth Grahame, author of *The Wind in the Willows*, are numerous. The enchanting illustrations for the book, drawn by E.H. Shepard, were based on this magnificent stretch of the river. Grahame spent most of his childhood at Cookham Dean and lived in Church Cottage, Pangbourne, in retirement until his death. Two notable attractions lie just to the north-west of **Lower Basildon**.

Basildon Park (N.T.) 2B

Open: *Apr–Oct, Wed–Sat 2–6, Sun, B.H. Mon 12–6. Closed Good Fri and the Wed following a B.H. Mon. Tel: Pangbourne (0734) 843040.*

Superbly set overlooking the Thames Valley, Basildon Park is an exceptional building of mellow Bath stone. Built in 1776, it stands in over 400 acres of parkland and woodland. The focal point of the interior is the unusual Octagon Room and there are fine paintings, furniture and plasterwork.

Beale Bird Park 2B

Open: *3 Mar–23 Dec 10–6. Tel: Pangbourne (0734) 845172.*

In an inviting riverside setting off the A324 is a 15-acre nature reserve – and much more! Established 33 years ago as the Child-Beale Wildlife Trust, the park now features an impressive collection of wildfowl, ornamental waterfowl and pheasants and other varieties of birds, many of them rare. There are also Highland cattle, rare sheep and llamas, a pets corner and a tropical house.

Most exhibits are along major walkways and the expanded Beale

The Dogs of Alcibiades, Basildon Park

Beale Bird Park

Centre offers educational and catering facilities and a year-round function room. There is a new 7¼in-gauge railway and children's play area and, in the summer months, 20-minute river trips.

David Simonds Wines
Talks and tastings of international wines are the specialities of David Simonds Wines, Buckhold Grange, Pangbourne. *Tel: Bradfield (0734) 744054.*

Westbury Farm Vineyard 2B
Tel: Pangbourne (0734) 843123.
The Romans once grew vines in the Thames Valley and in recent years the practice has been revived and several new vineyards established. Westbury Farm Vineyard is one notable example. The owner, Bernard Theobald, is the perfect host for an individual or group visit to this 14-acre vineyard and winery. Medieval barns have been converted for group tastings and talks on English wines. Day trout fishing is also available.

Reading
The county town of Royal Berkshire, Reading is a thriving centre of commerce and industry, with one of the best shopping centres in the south of England. Owing to its position where the River Kennet joins the Thames, it has a long and colourful history, first rising to importance during Norman times: Henry I founded an abbey here in 1121; interesting

Boulters Lock, near Maidenhead

ruins and one fine gateway remain. The Forbury Gardens, once the forecourt of the abbey, are an attractive floral focal point of the town.

The abbey ruins and gardens are linked by a short path to Chestnut Walk by the River Kennet, next to the prison which held Oscar Wilde. Look for walks signposted with the symbol of the reflected swan of the Reading Waterways Walk.

Reading has been university town since 1926 and the older university buildings in the town centre contrast vividly with the modern faculties and residence halls set among 300 acres of parkland at Whiteknights.

Blake's Lock Museum 3B
Open: *Mon–Fri 10–5, Sat, Sun 2–5, closed New Year's Day. Tel: Reading (0734) 590630.*
In Kenavon Drive off Forbury Road, about 15 minutes' walk from Reading town centre, is Blake's Lock Museum. Situated on the banks of the River Kennet in a Victorian pumping station, it features the town's waterways and many local trades and industries. There are also reconstructions of a printer's workshop, a bakery and a gentlemen's barber shop.

Cliveden, Taplow

Dinton Pastures Country Park 3B

Open: *Dawn–dusk. Tel: Twyford (0734) 342016.*
Just east of Reading between Woodley and Hurst off the B3030 is Dinton Pastures Country Park, 230 acres of lakes and fields with birdwatching, footpaths, watersports and coarse fishing. Visitors' Centre and ranger service.

The Hexagon 3B

Closed Aug. *Tel: Reading (0734) 591591.*
The Hexagon, Reading's unique multi-purpose entertainment centre, has an enviable reputation for top-quality performers, fine drama and interesting exhibitions.

Museum of English Rural Life 3B

Open: *Tue–Sat 10–1, 2–4.30. Tel: Reading (0734) 318663.*
A national collection of farm implements and domestic equipment depicting 150 years of country living is displayed at the Museum of English Rural Life on the University campus at Whiteknights.

36

Eight miles south of Reading on the Berkshire/Hampshire border are Wellington Country Park and Stratfield Saye House.

Stratfield Saye House 3C

Open: *May–Sept, daily except Fri 11.30–5. Tel: Basingstoke (0256) 882882.*
Just off the A33, Stratfield Saye dates from 1630 and was rebuilt in the reign of Charles I. It was presented by the nation to the first Duke of Wellington after his victory over Napoleon at Waterloo in 1815. The house contains many of the Great Duke's possessions, and his impressive funeral carriage is also displayed. The Wellington Exhibition in the stable block depicts his life and times. The gardens have been restored and the Pleasure Grounds contain rare trees, most of which were established by the 1st Duke.

Wellington Country Park 3C

Open: *Mar–Oct daily; Nov–Feb Sat, Sun 10–5.*
The park stands on a tract of more than 300 acres of woodland and reclaimed gravel workings and offers numerous opportunities for

entertainment and relaxation. There is a 35-acre lake with fishing, boat hire and sailboarding; nature trails and a deer park as well as a fitness course, adventure playground, animal farm and gift shop. Additional facilities include a miniature steam railway, the National Dairy Museum, woodland camping sites, riding school and the evolutionary Thames Time Trail.

Taplow

Cliveden (N.T.) 4B

Open: *Grounds: Mar–Dec, daily 11–6 (sunset if earlier); House: April–28 Oct, Thur, Sun 3–6, last admission 5.30. Tickets stating scheduled time of entry from information kiosk. Tel: Burnham (0628) 605069.*
Set on cliffs 200 feet above the Thames, the present house, built in 1851, was once the home of Nancy, Lady Astor, and is now let as a hotel to Blakeney Hotels Ltd, with three rooms open to visitors. The 375 acres of gardens and woodland include a magnificent parterre, a water garden and miles of woodland walks with spectacular views of the Thames.

Twyford

Rock's Country Wines 3B

Open: *Jan–16 Apr, Mon–Sat 10–5, Sun 12–4; 17 Apr–Dec, Mon–Sat 10–6, Sun 12–6. Tel: Twyford (0734) 342344.*

Directly off the A4 between Maidenhead and Reading at Twyford is Rock's Country Wines. Customers of this working winery are invited to taste free of charge and observe work in progress as English country wines and fruit wines are made to old cottage recipes, using modern methods and the fruits and flowers of the hedgerow, garden and orchard. Elderflower, raspberry and sparkling gooseberry wines are included in the range, as are Damson gin and plum brandy. There are a wine-maker's herb garden and an elderflower orchard.

Eton College

Windsor

Royal Windsor with its Castle and many other attractions has been the home and burial place of English kings and queens for 900 years.

In the centre of Windsor, a few yards from the Castle, stands the **Guildhall.** The building was begun in 1689 by Sir Thomas Fitch and completed after his death by Sir Christopher Wren. Note the colonnade of four pillars underneath, constructed as a joke by Wren so as *not* to support the council chamber above.

The river is the perfect vantage point from which to admire Windsor. Several boat operators run trips along this stretch of the Thames (see Leisure Afloat).

For those who want a bird's eye view of what Windsor has to offer, there are tours in open-top and replica 1920s buses (see Guided Tours).

Across a lovely old cast-iron footbridge from Windsor lies Eton and one of Britain's most famous schools, **Eton College.**

Duffey's Old Bakery 4B

Open: *Shop: Mon 6am–7pm, Sat 6–5, Sun 7–1. Tours by appointment. Tel: Windsor (0753) 865545.*

There is an opportunity to step back in time and experience the workings of a Victorian bakery at Duffey's Old Bakery in Oxford Road, Windsor. Groups and school parties may see bread and confectionary being handmade and baked in a traditional coal-fired oven.

Frogmore Gardens and Mausoleum 4B

Open: 2–3 May, 10.30–7 (last admission 6.30).
In the 400-acre Home Park south-east of Windsor Castle are Frogmore Gardens and the ornate mausoleum built by Queen Victoria for herself and her husband Prince Albert.

Museum of Ancient Wireless & Historic Gramophone Apparatus 4B

Open: by appointment. Tel: Slough (0753) 42242.
Two miles east of Windsor in Datchet is a small, private museum featuring vintage wireless, gramophone, phonograph, telephone wire- and tape-recording apparatus. The enthusiastic innovator Captain Maurice Seddon will share his considerable range of equipment and opinions (in any of five languages) with visitors.

Royalty and Empire Exhibition 4B

Open: daily 9.30–5.30 (4.30 winter). Closed 8–17 Jan. Tel: Windsor (0753) 857837.
In the Royalty and Empire Exhibition at the Central Station,

Madame Tussaud's has re-created the grand occasion of Queen Victoria's Diamond Jubilee in 1897 in its original surroundings. The royal train stands at the platform and on the parade ground 70 Coldstream Guards form a guard of honour. The climax of the exhibition is a breaktaking computerized theatre presentation, *Sixty Glorious Years*, which brings famous Victorians to life and depicts memorable events during Queen Victoria's long reign.

There are several interesting places to visit a short journey away from Windsor by car or bus. The 4,000 acres of Windsor Great Park used to be part of the great royal hunting forest. Although still Crown property, much of it is now open to the general public.

Savill Garden 4B

Open: daily (except 25–28 Dec) 10–6 or dusk. Tel: Egham (0784) 435544.
The Savill Garden, 35 acres of beautiful woodland containing rare trees, flowers and shrubs, is in Englefield Green, a few miles south of Windsor. It is justly famous for its rhododendrons, camellias, magnolias and hydrangeas, which give a glorious show of colour particularly in spring and summer.

Valley Gardens 4B

Open: daily 8–7. Tel: Windsor (0753) 860222.
A much larger, wilder tract, the Valley Gardens is on the north bank of Virginia Water. This 400-acre woodland garden contains a huge assortment of flowering trees and shrubs and several acres of grass, smothered by wild daffodils in the spring.

Windsor Castle 4B

Tel: Windsor (0753) 831118 for opening dates and times.
Windsor is one of the largest and oldest inhabited castles in the world. Though a fortress has existed here since the reign of William the Conqueror, much of what we see today, both inside and out, is the result of massive 19th-C. rebuilding by George IV. The Castle covers some 13 acres and its precincts are nearly a mile around.

The magnificent range of rooms that overlooks the Thames Valley and forms the State Apartments is largely the legacy of Charles II, who rebuilt the royal suite in the

Royalty and Empire

Guards at Windsor

The Round Tower,
Windsor Castle

1670s, and George IV, who 150 years later, spent a million pounds making these rooms even more splendid.

The State Apartments are open to the public unless the Queen is in residence. She uses them three times a year and for state visits, so it is advisable to check before travelling.

Next to the State Apartments is the entrance to Queen Mary's Dolls' House, designed by Sir Edwin Lutyens and given by the nation to Queen Mary in 1923.

St George's Chapel 4B

Open: *1–7 Jan, 3 Feb–Dec, Mon–Sat 10.45–3.45, Sun 2–3.45. Closed at other times on short notice. Tel: Windsor (0753) 865538.*
Within the Palace grounds, the Chapel is one of England's most superb ecclesiastical buildings. Although it has required major structural restoration since it was built between 1475–1528, today its soaring nave and many chapels are resplendent with stained glass, ornate woodwork, brass and elaborate masonry.

Ten monarchs lie buried here, including King Henry VIII and King George VI. The banners of the 26 Knights of the Garter hang in the choir.

Windsor Racecourse 4B

Open: *For details of meetings, send s.a.e. to The Racing Information Bureau, Winkfield Road, Ascot, Berks SL5 7HX. Tel: Ascot (0990) 25912.*

Windsor Safari Park 4B

Open: *daily from 10. Tel: Windsor (0753) 830886.*

Dolphins at Windsor Safari Park

An African theme runs through the numerous attractions at this park just 3½ miles from Windsor Castle on Winkfield Road. Lions, zebra, camels, elephants, baboons and giraffe roam in the drive-through game reserves, and throughout the day there is a programme of events featuring parrots, birds of prey, dolphins, sea-lions and Britain's only killer whale. Children especially enjoy the Adventure Playcentre, African Queen river boat ride, butterfly house and the Kilimanjaro Toboggan Run. There is a range of catering facilities.

The Chilterns

Buckinghamshire

Buckinghamshire has rightly been called the Queen of the Home Counties. From the Ouse and the Grand Union Canal in the north to the Thames in the south and the beechwoods of the Chiltern Hills in the east, it is a county with many gifts to share.

The Chilterns, running like a spine through the county, are known for their incomparable beechwoods – all that remains of a vast forest that once covered the whole county.

In the very centre of the county lies the Vale of Aylesbury with the county town of Aylesbury at its heart. This is rich, flat farmland with occasional sudden heights such as Brill Hill, The Clump at Quainton and Lodge Hill at Waddesdon to add drama to the landscape.

The Vale is one of the most picturesque parts of Buckinghamshire and richly studded with grand country houses. Indeed, Buckinghamshire has a generous share of historic houses for visitors to see, including several of the great homes of the Rothschild family, the most glorious of which must surely be Waddesdon Manor.

The northern part of the county is dominated by the new city of Milton Keynes, created around several towns and villages in 1967. The area's waterways – the Ouse, its tributary the Ouzel and the Grand Union Canal – provide many opportunities for riverside walks, watersports and angling.

Here too are some fine old towns, like Buckingham and Olney. Along the county's southern boundary the River Thames flows through some fine scenery. This is mainly residential, green-belt land, crossed by country roads and lanes with pretty villages, parks, heaths and woods. One of the most famous, Burnham Beeches near Stoke Poges, was a favourite haunt of the poet Thomas Gray.

Temple Bridge, Marlow

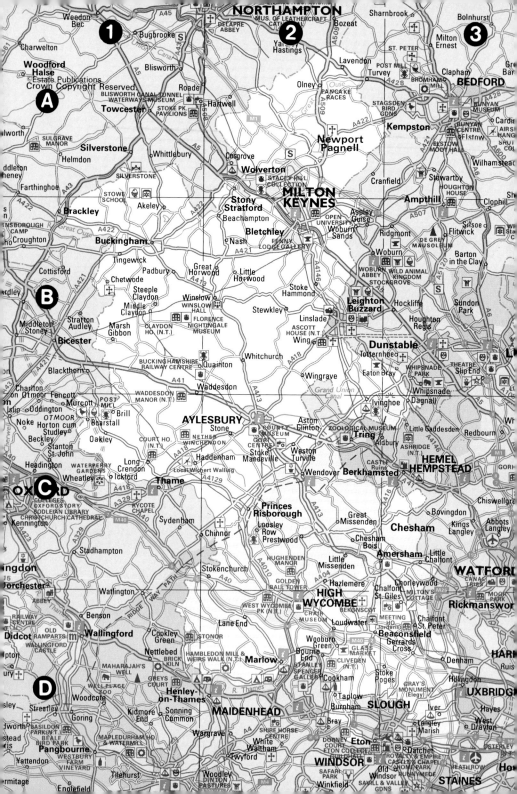

Amersham

Amersham Museum 3C

Temporarily closed. Tel: Amersham (0494) 725754 for 1990 re-opening date.
This local museum will reopen in the refurbished 15th-C. house at 49 High Street. The collection includes area artefacts from Roman times to the present with emphasis on local crafts and industries.

Aylesbury

Though it dates back to Anglo-Saxon times and has been the county town of Buckinghamshire since the reign of Henry VIII, Aylesbury town centre has a modern appearance.

Ascott House (N.T.) 2B

Open: House and Garden: 14 Apr–20 May, Tue–Sun and B.H. Mons (but closed Tue after B.H. Mons); 1–30 Sept, 2–6. Garden: Apr–Sept, every Wed and last Sun in each month; also 27 Aug, 2–6. Tel: Aylesbury (0296) 688242.
Ten miles north-east near Wing, this late-19th-C, half-timbered building is one of the Buckinghamshire homes of the Rothschild family. It has a fine Victorian garden and an outstanding collection of works of art, including important Dutch and English paintings, oriental porcelain and Chippendale furniture.

Buckinghamshire County Museum 2C

Open: Mon–Sat 10–1.30 and 2–5.
Closed Sun, New Year's Day, Good Fri, Christmas and Boxing Day. Tel: Aylesbury (0296) 82158.
Note: Due to a program of major refurbishment only the Aylesbury Gallery of local history and the Special Exhibition gallery will be open in 1990.
The County Museum in Church Street contains local history exhibits and is itself a classic example of 18th-C. architecture.

Waddesdon Manor

Bucks Goat Centre 2C

Open: daily 10–5. Tel: Stoke Mandeville (0296) 612983.
A few miles south-west, just outside Stoke Mandeville on the Old Risborough Road, you can watch the afternoon milking and the kids being fed at the Bucks Goat Centre. There are also free-range hens, sheep, turkeys and rabbits, and in the farm shop, goat cheeses, country cider and English wines are some of the specialities on sale. There is also a Gardening Corner for plants, shrubs and herbs.

Waddesdon Manor (N.T.) 1C

Open: House and Grounds: 4 Apr–28 Oct, Wed–Sun 1–5; May–Sept, Sat, Sun 1–6. House and Grounds open Good Fri and B.H. Mon 11–6. Bachelors' Wing open Fri, closed Good Fri. Grounds, aviary, Christmas shop and restaurant open 7 Nov–22 Dec, Wed–Sun 12–14. Tel: Aylesbury (0296) 651211.
Please note that children under 10 are not admitted to the house.
Just to the north of Aylesbury is Waddesdon Manor, built in 1874 for Baron Ferdinand de Rothschild in the style of a French château. Nowhere outside France are you likely to see such an impressive collection of 18th-C. French furniture, porcelain and Savonnerie carpets. There are also fine English portraits and objets d'art.

The Aylesbury Brewery Company has 186 public houses, mostly in Buckinghamshire but also spilling into adjacent counties. Several of its country inns offer especially good food. We would recommend the following: Weavers in Bierton Road, Aylesbury; The Dark Lantern just off Aylesbury's Market Square; Pettit's Wine Bar at the other end of the Market Square; The Horse and Jockey Motel in Buckingham Road, Aylesbury; The Chequers just outside Aylesbury at Weston Turville; The Wayfarer at Goldington, Bedford, a newly created hotel; and its elder sister in Brickhill Street, Milton Keynes, also called The Wayfarer. *Tel: Oxford (0865) 882255.*

43

Bekonscot Model Village

Beaconsfield

Bekonscot Model Village 3D

Open: *Mar–Oct, Mon–Fri 10–5; Sat, Sun 10–5.30.*
Tel: Beaconsfield (0494) 672919.
Warwick Road, Beaconsfield, is the home of the world's first model village. Now in its 61st year, this amazing miniature world includes a zoo (where you are asked not to feed the animals), a cinema, the minster with a stained-glass window by Edmund Dulac, a cricket match that is never interrupted by rain or bad light and an extensive railway serving seven stations. Its 1,200 hand-carved inhabitants also have use of a flying club, fishing village and lake. There are full-size refreshments, picnic and play areas for visitors' enjoyment.

The Glass Market 2D

Open: *Mon–Sat 9.30–5. Closed B.H. Mons. Tel: Beaconsfield (0494) 671033.*
Just across the M40 in rural surroundings at Wooburn Green, craftsmen at The Glass Market show visitors their skills in working with stained and other forms of decorative glass. Courses are also available and beautiful glass objects are on sale in the shop.

Penn Church 2C

About a mile north on the B474, the village of Penn stands high in the Chilterns, with views over the beechwoods. It was the home of numerous ancestors and descendants of the great Quaker William Penn, founder and first governor of Pennsylvania. The family is commemorated in the splendid Holy Trinity Church, parts of which date from Norman times. A fine medieval wall painting of the Last Judgement,

Brill Post Mill

restored following its discovery in 1938, is in the south aisle.

Brill

Brill Post Mill 1C

Open: *Easter–Sept, Sun 2.30–5.*
The Brill Post Mill stands out like a beacon. Built about 1680, it was in regular use until a few years ago. This is a good spot for picnics and kite-flying.

Boarstall Duck Decoy (N.T.) 1C

Open: *Good Fri–Aug B.H., Wed 2–5, Sat, Sun, B.H. Mon 10–5. Tel: Brill (0844) 237488.*
Just off the B4011 in 13 acres of woodland is a rare, 18th-C. duck decoy in working order. There is an information centre and a nature trail for visitors.

Palladian Bridge, Stowe Landscape Gardens

Buckingham

Alfred the Great named Buckingham the shire town in 866. It remained so until greatly damaged by fire in 1725; the rebuilding accounts for today's largely Georgian appearance.

Stowe School 1A

Open: *17 Mar–17 Apr, 7 Jul–4 Sept, daily 10–6 (last admission 5). Tel: Buckingham (0280) 813650.*
Now an independent school, this stately 18th-C. mansion three miles north-west of Buckingham was formerly the home of the Dukes of Buckingham and Chandos.

Stowe Landscape Gardens (N.T.) 1A

Open: *1–10 Jan, 17 Mar–17 Apr, 7 Jul–4 Sept, 15–31 Dec. Closed Good Fri, Christmas and Boxing Day. Tel: Buckingham (0280) 822850.*
The spectacular 350-acre gardens adjacent to Stowe School show the hand of some of England's foremost landscape gardeners: Bridgeman, Kent, Gibbs and 'Capability' Brown. They contain six lakes and 32 follies.

Chalfont St Giles

Chalfont Shire Horse Centre 3D

Open: *Apr–Sept daily 10–4. Tel: Chalfont St Giles (02407) 2304.*
Home of the mighty Chalfont Shires, the Centre has daily demonstrations at 11.30 and 2.30 as well as a children's play area, pets corner, display of vintage lorries, a shop and café. Its biggest attractions are, of course, the famous Shire horses which, when not at the Centre, appear around the country at shows, fetes and in films.

Chiltern Open Air Museum 3D

Open: *Apr–Oct, Wed, Sun, B.H. Mon 2–6; July–Aug, Wed–Sun 2–6. Tel: Chalfont St Giles (02407) 71117.*
16th–19th-C. Chiltern buildings rescued from demolition have been reconstructed in Newland Park, Gorelands Lane. As well as associated artefacts, there are regular displays of smithery, lace-making, bee-keeping and many other arts and crafts, a cafeteria and special events throughout the year.

Jordans Quaker Meeting House 3D

Open: *Mon 10–1, Sun, Wed–Sat 10–1, 2–6. Closes at dusk in winter. Meeting for worship Sun at 10.30. Tel: Chalfont St Giles (02407) 4146.*
The area around Jordans, south of Chalfont St Giles, is famous for its connections with the Society of Friends, also known as the Quakers. The Society was founded by George Fox around 1650 and the Friends' Meeting House was built here in 1688. It is still in use. William Penn, founder and first governor of Pennsylvania, lies in the nearby burial ground.

Judith Barratt Marketing of Pyghtle House, Misbourne Avenue, Gerrards Cross, Chalfont St Peter, Bucks, is a hotel and leisure specialist providing independent professional advice on operations, marketing and development. *Tel: Chalfont St Peter (02407) 2391.*

45

Old Jordans and Mayflower Barn 3D

Open: daily. Tel: Chalfont St Giles (02407) 4586 for enquiries and bookings for coffee, tea, lunch and dinner.

Old Jordans is a 17th-C. farmhouse where the early Quakers first held their meetings. Now owned by the Society of Friends, it is run as a centre for rest and inspiration for private guests and conferences. The Mayflower Barn was built in 1624 from timbers – alleged by some and hotly denied by others – to be taken from the ship which carried

Milton's Cottage

the Pilgrim Fathers to America in 1620.

Milton's Cottage 3D

Open: Mar–Oct, Tue–Sat and B.H. Mon 10–1, 2–6, Sun 2–6. Tel: Chalfont St Giles (02407) 2313.

The poet John Milton came to the village of Chalfont St Giles in 1665 to escape the plague and while here, completed his great work *Paradise Lost* and began *Paradise Regained*. The 16th-C. cottage in which he lived was bought by the people of the village in 1887 and has been open to the public ever since. It contains much

Milton memorabilia and a library including first and early editions. There is a charming cottage garden.

Dorney
Dorney Court 2D

Open: Good Fri, Easter Sat, Sun, Mon 2–5.30; Easter–May, Sun, B.H. Mon 2–5.30; June–Sept, Sun, Mon, Tue, 2–5.30. Last admission 5. Tel: Burnham (0628) 604638.

Just inside the county border, about five minutes from Eton on the B3026, lies one of England's finest Tudor manor houses. This enchanting pink-brick and timber house was built around 1500 and occupied by the Palmer family for nearly 400 years. The rooms contain early 15th- and 16th-C. oak and beautiful 17th-C. lacquer furniture, as well as family portraits, stained glass and needlework. Cheerful tea room.

High Wycombe
Hughenden Manor (N.T.) 2C

Open: Mar, Sat, Sun 2–6; Apr–Oct, Wed–Sat 2–6, Sun, B.H. Mon 12–6. Closed Good Fri. Tel: High Wycombe (0494) 32580.

Hughenden Manor, home of Benjamin Disraeli, lies in the valley 1½ miles north of High Wycombe on the A4128. The original house, mostly late 18th-C., was remodelled for Disraeli and his wife, who added an ornamental parapet, Gothic decorations and wallpapers which give the house its distinctive Victorian flavour. It has been extensively refurbished by the National Trust.

Brochure Display of Wye Estate, London Road, High Wycombe, offers a display and distribution service for leaflets and brochures with outlets in hotels, libraries and many other locations. Tel: High Wycombe (0494) 444967.

West Wycombe Park
(N.T.) 2D
Open: *Grounds: Apr, May, Sun, Weds, 2–6. Easter, May and Spring B.H., Sun and Mon 2–6. House and Grounds: June, July, Aug, Sun–Thur 2–6. Last admission 5.15. Tel: High Wycombe (0494) 24411.*
The Palladian mansion is mainly known as the home of Sir Francis Dashwood, the 18th-C. eccentric and dilettante. The house is richly decorated with frescoes and painted ceilings and has a fine collection of mirrors, furniture and pictures.

Wycombe Chair Museum 2D
Open: *Mon–Sat 10–1, 2–5. Closed B.H. Mon. Tel: High Wycombe (0494) 23879.*
High Wycombe has long been associated with chair and furniture making, beech from the surrounding woods being the basic material.
Set in gardens and housed in a 17th-C. building, Wycombe Chair Museum is devoted to the craft which has led to High Wycombe being known as 'Furniture Town'. Special emphasis on the Windsor chair; also cane and rush seating.

Ivinghoe
Pitstone Post Mill (N.T.) 3C
Open: *May–Sept, Sun, B.H. Mon 2.30–6. Last admission 5.30.*
One-half mile south of Ivinghoe and just west of the B488 stands Pitstone Post Mill. Two dates are carved on its timbers, the earlier – 1627 – making it the oldest dated mill in the country.

Midas Craft Fairs *9A Pack Horse Road, Gerrards Cross, Bucks. Tel: Gerrards Cross (0753) 886993.*
The organisers of quality craft fairs in venues such as Knebworth House and Mentmore Towers.

Temple of Music, West Wycombe Park

The West Wycombe Garden Centre (2C) on the
Chorley Road features a wide range of gardening supplies, plants and shrubs. There is also a shop and café.
Tel: High Wycombe (0494) 438635.

Marlow
This pleasant riverside town is most famous for the fine suspension bridge, designed by William Tierney Clark in 1832, which spans the river. Many fine Georgian houses line the streets and there is also the world-famous Compleat Angler Hotel, overlooking the long wier which runs down to Marlow Lock, an especially beautiful part of the Thames.

Chinese Room, Claydon House

Much of *Three Men in a Boat*, the comic novel set on the Thames, was written by Jerome K. Jerome while staying at the Two Brewers Inn.

Long Crendon
Long Crendon Courthouse (N.T.) 1C
Open: *Apr–Sept, Wed 2–6; Sat, Sun, B.H. Mon 11–6.*
West of Aylesbury is the ancient village of Long Crendon. The 14th-C. building in which the manorial courts were held from the time of Henry V until recently is preserved by the National Trust.

Middle Claydon
Claydon House (N.T.) 1B
Open: *Apr–Oct, Sat–Wed 2–6, B.H. Mon 1–6. Closed Good Fri. Tel: Steeple Claydon (029 673) 349/693.*
Claydon House at Middle Claydon (13 miles north-west of Aylesbury) is chiefly known for its close associations with Florence Nightingale, who stayed there for long periods whilst visiting her sister. Her bedroom, sitting-room and a museum containing mementoes of her life are displayed.
The stone-faced house is, in fact, the one remaining wing of a beautifully proportioned 18th-C. house and contains several extravagantly redecorated rooms. There is an intricate wrought-iron staircase under a glazed oval dome, and a Chinese tearoom!

47

Milton Keynes

Begun in 1967, Milton Keynes is a monument to modern urban planning. Cycleways and sweeping green spaces complement the modern building materials, and care has been taken to blend the old with the new. In Central Milton Keynes is one of Europe's largest covered shopping areas where two main landscaped arcades house a range of stores that attracts shoppers from miles around. There are also excellent leisure and recreational facilities.

The market town of Bletchley, the railway centre of Wolverton, and Stony Stratford with its Georgian High Street have all been allowed to keep their individuality in this new urban complex.

Visit the field centre for archaeology and ecology on the site of a 12th-C. priory at Bradwell, the first Peace Pagoda in the western hemisphere sited at Willen Lake, and the world-famous concrete cows at Monks Way, also in Bradwell.

Bradwell Tower Mill 2A

Open: *exterior at any time.*
Off the A422 at Bradwell in northern Milton Keynes is the Bradwell Tower Mill. Built with spring sails in 1816, the mill has been restored by the Milton Keynes Development Corporation.

Fenny Lodge Gallery 2B

Open: *Mon–Fri 9–5, Sat 9–4. Closed B.H. Tel: Milton Keynes (0908) 642207.*
Fenny Lock on the Grand Union Canal is the attractive setting of Fenny Lodge Gallery. In this beautiful 18th-C. house, with gardens sweeping down to the waterside, you will discover an exciting selection of graphic arts, embroideries, collages, ceramics, sculpture, turned and carved wood, free-blown and stained glass, rushwork and jewellery.

48

Peace Pagoda, Milton Keynes

Stacey Hill Museum 2A

Open: *May–Oct, first and third Sun in each month, B.H. Mon 2–5. Working weekends: 20, 21 May, 16, 17 Sept. Tel: Milton Keynes (0908) 312270.*
Stacey Hill Farm on Southern Way, Wolverton, has a wonderful collection of bygones of North Bucks life, including carriages, agricultural machinery and domestic items, including photographic equipment and radios.

Olney

The Shrove Tuesday pancake race has been a tradition at Olney since 1445.

Nowadays the Pancake Bell still rings at 11.55 each Shrove Tuesday to summon competitors to run the 415-yard course between the Market Place and the church, tossing their pancakes three times. The shriving service follows the race at midday.

Princes Risborough

Lacey Green Windmill 2C

Open: *May–Sept, Sun, B.H. Mon 3–6.*
The mill is 1½ miles south at Windmill Farm, Lacey Green. Built in 1650, it is probably Britain's oldest surviving 'smock' mill (one with a fixed base on which the cap and sails rotate). It has been diligently restored with the original wooden machinery by The Chiltern Society.

Quainton

Six miles north-west of Aylesbury,
the village of Quainton has a
sloping green, an ancient market
cross, a restored windmill,
attractive 17th-C. almshouses and
an interesting church, but it is
probably best known for the
Buckinghamshire Railway Centre,
housed at the former Quainton
Road Station a mile from the
village.

Buckinghamshire Railway Centre 2B

Open: *In steam: Apr–Oct, Sun,
B.H. Mon; and Wed in June–Aug
11–6. Static viewing: June–Aug,
Thur, Fri, Sat 11–6. Tel: Quainton
(029 675) 450.*

The Centre is Britain's largest
private railway collection, packed
with dozens of engines and rolling
stock. Its treasures range from the
Great Western Railway's crack
express engine *King Edward I* to
the tiny Number 1900, Britain's
smallest standard-gauge steam
engine. The entire family can
experience the thrill of rail travel in
the Victorian age with rides in a
vintage steam train, or simply
savour the atmosphere of bygone
days in the restored country
station.

Quainton Tower Mill 2B

Open: *Sun 10–1.*
On the village green, this 70-foot
tower mill is the tallest in
Buckinghamshire. Built in the
18th-C., the mill is being restored
by The Quainton Windmill
Society.

Stoke Poges

To the south of the M40
motorway, in the county's south-
east corner, is the village of Stoke
Poges which, together with its
famous churchyard, will always be
associated with the poet Thomas
Gray and his *Elegy Written in a
Country Churchyard.* Nearby, the
70 acres of Burnham Beeches,
given for public use in 1880,
provide woodland walks along

well-defined paths and scenic
drives.

St. Peter and St. Paul's, Olney

Knebworth House

Hertfordshire

Hertfordshire offers visitors the best of the old and the excitement of the new. You may wander through pretty showpiece villages like Much Hadham or Aldbury, explore the remains of a unique Roman theatre or, for contrast, delight in the green spaciousness of England's first 'garden city' – all within the borders of this inviting county.

Its many bustling towns and cities are surrounded by large areas of unspoiled countryside, much of which is accessible to the public. The peace of thickly wooded hillsides and parkland, gently sloping farmland crossed by rivers, streams and lakes contrasts with thriving centres of population. The Grand Union Canal in the east and the Lee and Stort Navigation in the west give access to hundreds of miles of recreational waterways (see Leisure Afloat). Among the many open areas to enjoy are the Colne Valley Park, stretching west towards Rickmansworth, and the Lee Valley Regional Park in the east, where leisure facilities have been developed along the river valley as far as London.

Hertfordshire echoes with numerous historic associations: William the Conqueror was offered the English Crown in Berkhamsted; Edmund Tudor, father of the first Tudor king, was born at Much Hadham; Hatfield was the childhood home of Elizabeth I. There are many fine historic houses to visit as well, such as Knebworth, with its spectacular Victorian-Gothic façade, and the Jacobean Hatfield House. The great writer and playwright George Bernard Shaw also chose to live in Hertfordshire; at Ayot St Lawrence his home remains much as it was during his lifetime.

There are ancient towns and cities, each with its unique story to tell: Baldock, Hitchin, Bishop's Stortford, Hemel Hempstead and, of course, St Albans all contain worthwhile sights. Near the turn of this century, however, the county also became the home of Britain's Garden City and New Town projects which revolutionized urban living patterns. Letchworth was first, followed in 20 years by Welwyn Garden City and still later by Stevenage, Hatfield and Hemel Hempstead.

Hatfield House

Aldbury

Just east of Tring, this picture-postcard spot with its half-timbered houses grouped around the green and duck pond is often featured in television programmes and films depicting the archetypal English village.

The Country Shop (1B)

Open: *Tue–Sat, B.H. Mon 10.30–5.30, Sun 11–5.30.* Tel: *Aldbury Common (044 285) 251.*
This cosy little shop at 14 Trooper Road offers a wide selection of British (and especially local) handiwork, country crafts and gifts.

Ashwell

Ashwell Village Museum 3A

Open: *Sun, B.H. Mon 2.30–5.* Tel: *Ashwell (09174) 2155.*
In the village of Ashwell north of Baldock is a charming folk museum housed in a timber-framed medieval building. There are many other historic buildings in the village.

Ayot St Lawrence

Shaw's Corner (N.T.) 2B

Open: *Apr–Oct, Wed–Sat 2–6; Sun, B.H. Mon 12–6. Closed Good Fri. Tel: Stevenage (0438) 820307.*
In the small village of Ayot St Lawrence, tucked away in an angle of a leafy lane, is Shaws Corner, home of the playwright and author George Bernard Shaw from 1906 until his death in 1950. Several rooms remain as they were in his lifetime, with his hats hanging in the hall and his pens lying on the desk. The summerhouse where he did his writing stands at the bottom of the garden.

Berkhamsted

Ashridge Estate (N.T.) 1B

Monument, shop and National Trust information centre
Open: *Apr–Oct, Mon–Thur 2–5, Sat, Sun B.H. 2–5.30.*
Two miles north of Berkhamsted, just off the B4506, the Ashridge Estate stretches across 4,000 acres including five commons, woodlands and the hills up to Ivinghoe Beacon. The granite monument was erected in 1832 to commemorate the canal-building feats of the 3rd Duke of Bridgewater.

Ashridge House Gardens (N.T.) 1B

Open: *Apr–Oct, Sat, Sun 2–6, House: open some weekends. Tel: Little Gaddesden (044284) 3491.*
The house, in early Gothic-Revival style, was begun in 1808 by James Wyatt for the 7th Earl of Bridgewater. The many small surrounding gardens were the creations of Humphrey Repton in 1813.

Berkhamsted Castle (E.H.) 1B

Open: *any reasonable time.*
Little remains of the Norman castle which was once a favourite royal residence. It was here in 1066 that William the Conqueror received a deputation of Saxon nobles who offered him the English Crown.

Dockey Wood, Ashridge

The surviving wing of the Royal Palace at Hatfield

Bishop's Stortford

Bishop's Stortford is a thriving market town and shopping centre. The River Stort runs through its centre, forming a pleasant conservation area where passenger boat trips are available (see Leisure Afloat).

The Lee and Stort Navigation reaches into the middle of Bishop's Stortford and you can bring a boat all the way here from the Thames (see Leisure Afloat). Hatfield Forest, three miles east of Bishop's Stortford, has a variety of wildlife including fallow deer, badgers, and pike and tench in the lake. There are boats for hire and a nature trail.

Rhodes Memorial Museum and Commonwealth Centre 4B

Open: *Tue–Sat 10–4. Closed B.H. Mon and the first two weeks of August. Tel: Bishop's Stortford (0279) 651746.*

In South Road, Bishop's Stortford, is the house where Cecil

Rhodes was born in 1853. It's now a museum with 15 rooms devoted to Rhodes' life and work in all parts of southern Africa.

Broxbourne

Broxbourne Lido 3B

Open: *daily; closed for several weeks around Christmas. Tel: Hoddesdon (0992) 446677.*

The riverside complex at Broxbourne Lido includes a leisure centre and wave machine, picnic area and riverside terraces. Boats are for hire and there are self-catering chalets for fishermen.

Paradise Park 3B

Open: *daily 10–6 (dusk in winter). Last admission 5. Tel: Hoddesdon (0992) 468001.*

Two miles west off the A1170 on Bell Lane is Paradise Park, a woodland zoo and pleasure park. The 25-acre zoo has a wide variety of animals, some roaming free. There are rides for small children, a miniature train and crazy golf.

Lee Valley Park 3B/C

Tel: Lea Valley (0992) 717711.
Broxbourne is also the headquarters of the Lee Valley Park Authority, which is integrating the leisure facilities of the River Lee from Stanstead Abbots to Newham in London. There is an exciting range of camping and caravan sites, sailing and riding centres and two working farms open to visitors.

Hatfield

Hatfield House 3B

Open: *25 Mar–14 Oct. House: Tue–Sat 12–4.15, Sun 1.30–5, B.H. Mon 11–5; Gardens: daily 11–6. Tel: Hatfield (0707) 262823.*

Dominating the nearby hillside village of Old Hatfield is Hatfield House with its magnificent gardens. Two miles east of the A1(M), this celebrated Jacobean House was built for Robert Cecil, first Earl of Salisbury and Chief Minister to King James I, and has

54

Rampage Sports Promotions at Elstree
Aerodrome, Borehamwood, offers a full range of business promotions and incentives. They feature a selection of All-Terrain Vehicles for extrovert hospitality. Tel: (01 207) 6060.

been the home of the Cecil family since 1611. The staterooms are rich in world-famous paintings and fine furniture. In the delightful gardens stands the surviving wing of the Royal Palace of Hatfield where Elizabeth I spent much of her girlhood and held her first Council of State in 1558. Medieval banquets are held on most nights of the week.

The National Patchwork Championships will be held here 5–8 July.

Mill Green Museum and Watermill 3B
Open: *Tue–Fri 10–5, Sat, Sun, B.H. Mon 2–5. Tel: Hatfield (0707) 271362.*
Standing on the River Lee, on the northern side of the A1000/A414 junction, this 18th-C. mill has been extensively restored and a new water wheel installed. Flour is produced in the traditional way and used to make the Mill Green Loaf. The adjoining miller's house is a small local history museum with changing exhibitions and summer craft demonstrations.

Hemel Hempstead
The old town of Hemel Hempstead dates from before the Norman Conquest and several Tudor houses may be seen in the High Street. The graceful spire of St Mary's, said to be the county's most complete Norman church, dominates the scene. The new town dates from 1947 and has a central shopping area adjoining attractive water gardens.

Hemel Hempstead Arts Centre 2B
Open: *Mon–Sat 10–5. Closed B.H. Mon, Christmas, Boxing Day, New Year's Day. Tel: Hemel Hempstead (0442) 42827.*
The Old Town Hall in High Street is the home of the Hemel Hempstead Arts Centre. In addition to weekly theatre upstairs, there is a very pleasant bistro, a cabaret in the cellar, films and musical events.

Hertford
Four rivers come together at Hertford: the Lee, Beane,

The Marble Hall, Hatfield House

Mimram and Rib. Indeed the town marks the highest navigable point of the River Lee. The 28-mile Lee Navigation runs from here through the loveliest parts of the Lee Valley into the Thames east of the Isle of Dogs, providing, with its barges and small boats, one of this area's most scenic features.

Hertford is an attractive and ancient small county town. There was a thriving community here long before the Romans came and the Saxons made it their capital. In recent times, the town has become known as an antiques centre, with many fascinating antiques shops in and around St Andrew's Street.

Hertford Castle 3B

Open: *May–Sept, the first Sun in each month 2.30–4.30. Grounds open daily all year.*

The centre of Hertford was shaped around the castle (occupied for nearly 1,000 years), the remains of which can still be visited. In the grounds are 18th-C. round towers, a massive 12th-C. curtain wall and the 15th-C. gatehouse. This gatehouse, known as The Castle, features intricate brickwork and timber, especially in the Mayor's Parlour and Robing Room.

Hertford Museum 3B

Open: *Tue–Sat 10–5. Closed 23–26 Dec and Good Fri. Tel: Hertford (0992) 582686.*
Housed in a 17th-C. building at 18 Bull Plain, the museum has displays of local geology, archaeology and natural history. A 17th-C. knot garden and special Hertfordshire gallery are planned.

Hitchin

In the north-west of the county, Hitchin has many well-preserved ancient buildings. The cathedral-like 12th-C. parish church of St Mary and the Priory are both worth a visit. There are also many beautiful old houses in Sun Street,

River Lea

London Country Bus (North West) Ltd.

operates services in south-west Hertfordshire as well as south Buckinghamshire, east Berkshire and north-west London. They offer daily service between High Wycombe/Beaconsfield and Heathrow, with connections to Gatwick and Luton, as well as reduced-rate period travel passes in some areas. *For enquiries please call you nearest local office on: Watford (0923) 673121; Amersham (0494) 216934; Slough (0753) 24144; Hemel Hempstead (0442) 216934.*

High Street, Old Tilehouse Street and Bucklersbury.

Hitchin Museum and Art Gallery 2A

Open: *Mon–Sat 10–5, closed B.H. Mon. Tel: Hitchin (0462) 34476.*
Hitchin Museum and Art Gallery contains exhibits of local interest, including agricultural, straw-plaiting, costume and textiles, brewing and natural history. It is also the regimental museum of the Hertfordshire Yeomanry.

Letchworth

Letchworth First Garden City Museum 3A

Open: *Mon–Fri 2–4.30, Sat 10–1, 2–4. Tel: Letchworth (0462) 683149.*
The First Garden City Museum at 296 Norton Way South charts the history of the 'garden city' movement and the social history of Letchworth.

Created in 1903 by visionary town planner Sir Ebenezer Howard, many of Letchworth's city-centre innovations are now common features in British towns.

Letchworth Museum and Art Gallery 3A

Open: *Mon–Sat 10–5. Closed B.H. Tel: Letchworth (0462) 685647.*
Letchworth Museum and Art Gallery has exhibits featuring natural history, archaeology and the history of man in north Hertfordshire.

Much Hadham

One of the loveliest villages in Hertfordshire, Much Hadham stands in the Ash Valley between Ware and Bishop's Stortford. It is a village with distinguished historical connections: Edmund

Tudor, father of the Tudor monarchs, was born here and it was here that the bishops of London had their summer palace. Parts of the 600-year-old palace still stand.

Rickmansworth

Moor Park Mansion 2C
Open: *Mon–Fri 10–12, 2.30–4, Sat 10–12. Closed B.H. Tel: Rickmansworth (0923) 773146.*
Set in parkland south-east of Rickmansworth is Moor Park, acknowledged to be the grandest 18th-C. mansion in Hertfordshire.

Reconstructed in Palladian style, the spectacular interior painting is the work of Sir James Thornhill, who painted the dome of St Paul's.

Rickmansworth Aquadrome 2C
Open: *daily. Tel: Rickmansworth (0923) 776611.*
At Rickmansworth Aquadrome there are fine water-sports facilities as well as a lakeside picnic site, children's play equipment, woodland walks and fishing in season. Colne Valley Regional Park, a popular centre for countryside recreation, and Chorleywood Common are also nearby.

Royston

Royston is said to have been named after the Lady Roysia who placed a cross set in stone to mark the crossing of Ermine Street and Icknield Way many centuries ago. The stone is still there, and so too are many of Royston's ancient buildings.

Royston Cave 3A
Open: *Easter–Sept, Sat, Sun, B.H. Mon 2.30–5, by appointment. Tel: Royston (0763) 242002.*
One of Royston's unusual features is the large bell-shaped cave under Melbourn Street. It is of uncertain origin, but thought to be pre-Roman and contains medieval carvings.

Royston Museum 3A
Open: *Wed, Thur, Sat 10–5. Tel: Royston (0763) 42587.*
This small local-history museum in Lower King Street mounts regularly changing exhibitions.

St Albans

As Verulamium, St Albans was one of the leading cities of the Roman Empire. Named for the first Christian martyr in Britain, Alban, who was executed about AD209, St Albans has developed around the magnificent Cathedral and Abbey Church of St Alban.

Around the field from the abbey gateway stands the Old Fighting Cocks Inn, whose triangular shape derives from its use in the past as a cockpit. The city streets, notably Fishpool Street and George Street, contain some beautiful old houses, many of them excellently restored, some dating back to the 15th C.

Cathedral and Abbey Church of St Alban 2B
Open: *daily May–Sept until 6.45, Oct–Apr until 5.45. Tel: St Albans (0727) 60780.*
Though originally built by the Saxons on the supposed site of St Alban's execution, the abbey we see today is Norman with 12th- and 13th-C. additions, making it the second-longest church in England. It became a cathedral in 1877. The magnificent new Laporte rose window was unveiled in the north transept last year by H.R.H. The Princess of Wales. The Chapter House was opened in 1982 and houses the shop and Refectory café.

The massive abbey gateway, once the main entrance to the Benedictine monastery, is now all that remains of the buildings to the south.

Cathedral and Abbey Church of St Alban

Roman remains at Verulamium

Museum of St Albans 2B

Open: *Mon–Sat 10–5, Sun, B.H. 2–5. Tel: St Albans (0727) 56679.*
This recently redesigned local history museum in Hatfield Road tells the story of St Albans from the dissolution of the monasteries to the present. It also houses a nationally recognized collection of local craft tools displayed in reconstructed workshops.

Clock Tower 2B

Open: *Good Fri–mid Sept, Sat, Sun, B.H. Mon 10.30–5. Tel: St Albans (0727) 60984.*
At the Market Cross in the High Street stands a five-storey, 15th-C. flint and rubble clock tower. There are fine views from the roof, a small exhibition of local history and the 1866 clockworks can be seen.

Gardens of the Rose 2C

Open: *16 June–21 Oct, Mon–Sat 9–5, Sun, B.H. Mon 10–6. Tel: St Albans (0727) 50461.*
South of St Albans in Chiswell Green Lane are the world-renowned Royal National Rose Society's gardens. Thirty thousand roses of 1,700 varieties are displayed in 12 acres. Especially
58

interesting are the trial grounds where new varieties, submitted by leading hybridists from all over the world, undergo field trials. Each year in July there is a major festival to coincide with the best of the rose flowerings.

Verulamium Museum 2B

Open: *Apr–Oct, Mon–Sat 10–5.30, Sun 2–5.30; Oct–Feb closes at 4. Tel: St Albans (0727) 66100.*
Relics of the city's past are found in the Verulamium Museum, including late Iron Age and Roman material, superb mosaics and a wide range of pottery. New exhibitions showing 400 years of domestic life in Verulamium open at Easter. In the nearby park is the hypocaust – one room of the bath wing of a Roman town house. Large sections of the Roman wall can also still be seen in the park which has a lake, children's amusements, sports facilities and views of the cathedral.

Verulamium Roman Theatre 2B

Open: *daily 10–5 (dusk in winter). Closed Christmas and Boxing Day.*
West of St Albans in the grounds

of the Gorhambury Estate is the Roman theatre, unique in Britain in having a raised stage unlike an amphitheatre. Not discovered until 1847, the theatre is thought to have built around AD 150 and is the only completely exposed Roman theatre in Britain.

Aylett Nurseries (2C)

famous for their award-winning dahlias, is conveniently located on the eastbound A414 near London Colney just outside St Albans. They will help you design (or redesign) your garden and offer a vast selection of plants, trees and shrubs, as well as garden tools, furniture and equipment. *Tel: Bowmansgreen (0702) 22255.*

Stevenage

Stevenage, just off the A1(M), was the first of the post-war "new towns". The town centre is for pedestrians only, with canopied streets, attractive squares and a very well-equipped leisure centre which is also the home of a local theatre. The original town is to the

Roger Harvey Garden Centre (3B) is

housed in attractively converted historic farm buildings at Bragbury End near Stevenage. In addition to an outstanding selection of indoor and outdoor plants and shrubs, garden equipment and furniture, the centre has a children's play area and pets corner, café and even tanks of exotic fish. *Tel: Stevenage (0438) 811777.*

north with numerous old coaching inns along the High Street.

Benington Lordship Gardens 3B

Open: *Feb, Sun, Wed 12–5 (for snowdrops); Easter, Spring and Summer B.H. Mons 12–5; May–Aug Wed, Sun 12–5, and Wed in Apr and Sept 12–5.*

Fives miles east of Stevenage in the village of Benington are these beautiful, old-fashioned gardens. There are sheets of snowdrops, scillas and spring flowers, as well as double herbaceous borders, masses of roses, shrubs and trees. Spread over seven acres, the gardens nestle into the hillside on the site of a Norman castle overlooking lakes and parkland.

Benington Lordship

There is a small plant centre open in summer.

Cromer Post Mill 3A

Open: *exterior at any time.*
Cromer is about five miles north-east of Stevenage. North-east again, on the B1037, stands this restored, 17th-C. windmill.

Fairlands Valley Park 3B

Open: *daily.*
At Six Hills Way, this 150-acre park has one lake for sailing and fishing and a smaller one for rowing, model craft and paddle boats. There are also paddling pools and horse riding.

Knebworth House 3B

Open: *7 Apr–20 May Sat, Sun, B.H. Mon and school holidays; 26 May–28 June and 3 July–9 Sept Sat, Sun, Tue-Fri; 15–30 Sept Sat, Sun. Park and Playground 11–5.30; House and Gardens 12–5. Tel: Stevenage (0438) 812661.*
1990 marks the 500th year that Knebworth House has been the family home of the Lyttons. Just south-west of Stevenage on the west side of the A1 (M), the house owes much of its splendid Gothic exterior to Victorian romantic novelist and statesman Sir Edward Bulwer-Lytton. Stucco and ornate Gothic decoration conceal the red

brick and simple lines of the original Tudor house. The beautiful gardens, relaid by Sir Edwin Lutyens in 1909, are now restored to their Edwardian glory. The 250 acres of parkland surrounding the house include an adventure playground, narrow-gauge railway, The Barns Restaurant and other attractions.

Stevenage Museum 3B

Open: *Mon–Sat 10–5. Tel Stevenage (0438) 354292.*
The excellent museum in St George's Way concentrates on local and natural history, with live exhibits and aquaria. They have recently acquired a large find of Roman coins.

Tring

Zoological Museum, 1B

Open: *Mon–Sat 10–5, Sun 2–5. Closed New Year's Day, Good Fri, May Day and 24–26 Dec. Tel: Tring (044 282) 4181.*
Tucked into a fold of the wooded Chilterns lies Tring, where the world-famous zoological museum was established by Lord Lionel Walter Rothschild. It retains much of its original charm and atmosphere and contains a magnificent collection of animals from dressed fleas to domestic dogs. There is a picnic site in the gardens.

Zoological Museum, Tring

Waltham Cross

Waltham Cross was named after the famous Eleanor Cross, erected in 1291 by Edward I to mark the route taken by his wife's funeral cortège to Westminster Abbey. Nearby are Waltham Abbey and Gardens, dating from 1177.

Champneys at Tring
(1B) provides a comprehensive, sound program for fitness and well-being. Counseling, sporting and social activities, and fine calorie-controlled cuisine are available in the luxury of Champneys' 170-acre parkland estate. *Tel: Tring (0442) 863351.*

Capel Manor Horticultural and Environmental Centre
3C
Open: *Apr–Oct, Mon–Fri 10–4.30, Sat, Sun 10–5.30; Oct–Mar, Mon–Fri 10–4.30.*
Set in the grounds of the beautiful Capel Estate, Bullsmore Lane, are 30 acres of ornamental and educational gardens, including period gardens and those for the disabled, many water features and an Italian-style maze. The centre also offers a variety of horticultural courses and a schools liaison service. *Tel: Lea Valley (0992) 763849.*

Ware
Once a prosperous centre of the malting industry, Ware stands on the River Lee on the route from London to Cambridge. Many of its buildings and streets are of historic interest, including the manor

house in Priory Park. Alas, the famous Great Bed of Ware, mentioned by Shakespeare in *Twelfth Night*, is now in the Victoria and Albert Museum.
  This stretch of the River Lee is a special attraction with its many colourful narrowboats and 18th-C. gazebos on its banks.

Van Hage's Garden Centre (3B) on the
A1170 at Great Amwell near Ware has grown into a star attraction. Set in 125 acres, it can provide your every gardening need, from plants, trees and shrubs to complete garden 'blueprints' and sample display gardens. There is also a café, small children's farm and a miniature railway. *Tel: Ware (0920) 870811.*

Welwyn Garden City

Welwyn Garden City, the second of Ebenezer Howard's garden cities, was developed in 1920.

Two large areas of parkland close to Welwyn Garden City are open to the public. Sherrardspark Wood offers woodland walks and a nature trail in its 170 acres. Stanborough Park is rapidly becoming established as a major attraction for visitors. As well as beautiful surroundings, the park offers facilities for many water sports, including sailing, windsurfing and boating.

Christine Akehurst
Tel: Cuffley (0707) 42126.
One of Britain's few professional lady toastmasters is available to give that special touch to any occasion, from large business gatherings to small private functions.

Watford

Watford, Hertfordshire's largest town, presents a busy and prosperous appearance to the visitor with modern shops, a large residential area and a thriving commercial life. The Palace Theatre has the distinction of being the only professional theatre in the county.

The Grand Union Canal winds its way through Watford's Cassiobury Park. This was the creation of the Earl of Essex, the landowner 18th-C. who insisted that the canal should be pleasing to the eye, with an ornamental stone bridge as its highlight. Today the park is a popular place for recreation with open spaces, footpaths and various sporting facilities, plus a mini railway and paddling pools. You can also enjoy a narrowboat canal trip from here in summer (see Leisure Afloat).

Cheslyn Gardens 2C

Open: *daily, Apr–Sept 9–8, Oct–Mar 9–4.*
Cheslyn Gardens in Nascot Wood Road offer the visitor the

Arcturus, Cassiobury Park, Watford

opportunity to explore interesting woodland gardens with a large variety of rare plants, trees and shrubs, as well as an aviary and ornamental pond.

There are more pleasant walks to be found at Whippendell Woods in Grove Lane, especially when the many bluebells are in bloom.

Shaw's Corner, Ayot St Lawrence

Watford Museum 2C

Open: *Mon–Sat 10–5. Tel: Watford (0923) 32297.*
Built in 1775, the museum has displays of local history, with the emphasis on printing and brewing, as well as a picture gallery, special exhibitions, and local history publications.

Minster Lovell Hall

Oxfordshire

The colourful history and satisfying scenery of Oxfordshire are closely linked in today's landscape. Prehistoric man, Romans, Saxons and Normans had all left their imprint by the time the medieval wool merchants endowed magnificent churches with the profits of their trade, and for at least seven centuries scholars have explored and extended the boundaries of knowledge at Oxford. This extraordinary city combines the bustle of the marketplace with the hush of a monastery; the crackle of the new with the quiet confidence of the well-established; and the cutting edge of research with the patient knowledge of centuries.

Many of the county's other towns and villages have a claim to fame as well: Wantage was the birthplace of King Alfred; Banbury is famous as the home of its cakes, cattle and the cross of the 'Ride a cock horse' nursery rhyme;

and Winston Churchill was born at Blenheim Palace and lies buried at Bladon near Woodstock. As if this weren't enough, there is also an estate-sized wildlife park near Burford, an intriguing steam railway centre at Didcot and at Witney, a farm museum where the clock is always turned back to the hard work and country pleasures of Edwardian times.

Finally, there is the steady River Thames, wending its way through lush countryside and delightful waterside towns, gathering momentum on its journey towards London. Every summer Henley-on-Thames hosts England's best-known regatta and graceful punts ply Oxford's waterways. Despite its distance from the sea, Oxfordshire, with its many lovely rivers and the Oxford Canal, provides ample opportunities for relaxation afloat.

Wittenham Clumps, near Abingdon

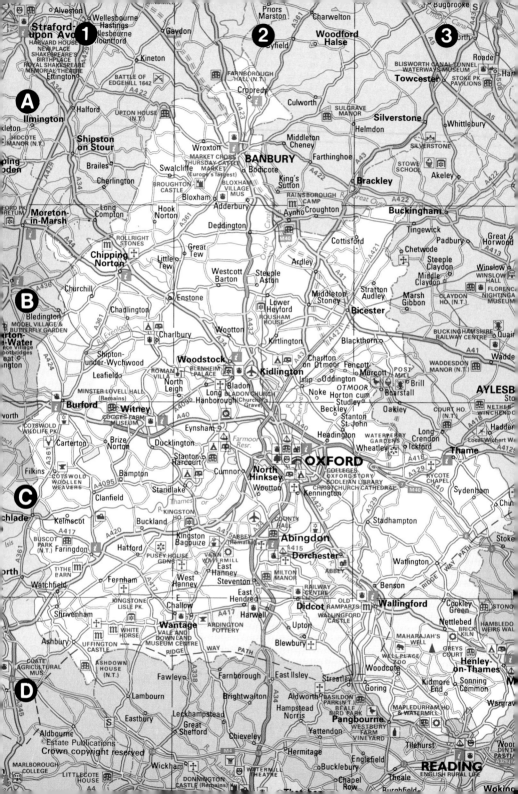

Abingdon

Abingdon offers visitors riverside walks, good moorings, and boat hire, including daily summer boat trips to Oxford and back. Abingdon Boat Centre, operating from quaintly named Nag's Head Island, offers river trips and boats for hire (see Leisure Afloat).

An imposing Napoleonic prison beside the Thames has been imaginatively converted into a busy leisure centre, known as the Old Gaol.

River Thames at Abingdon

Abbey Buildings 2C

Open: *Apr–Sept, Tue–Sun 2–6; Oct–Mar, Tue–Sun 2–4. Tel: Abingdon (0235) 25339.*
Abingdon's origins date from its abbey, circa AD 675. In Thames Street some of the adjacent buildings and the remains of England's third-largest abbey can still be visited.

County Hall and Museum 2C

Open: *Apr–Sept, Tue–Sun 1–5; Oct–Mar, Tue–Sun 1–4. Tel: Abingdon (0235) 23703.*
The delightful old County Hall in the Market Place – a reminder that Abingdon was once the county town of Berkshire – was built in the late 17th C. by one of Wren's

masons, Christopher Kempster of Burford. It now houses the town museum.

Long Alley Almshouses 2C

Open: *exterior at any time.*
The Long Alley Almshouses behind St Helen's church in Abingdon date from the 15th C. and are still in use.

Milton Manor 2C

Open: *Easter–Oct, Sat, Sun, B.H. Mon 2–5.30. Tel: Abingdon (0235) 831871/831287.*
Milton Manor House, south of Abingdon, is a delightful 17th-C. house designed by Inigo Jones and later enlarged by the addition of Georgian wings. It stands in 20 acres of garden beside a lake. The house is notable for its Strawberry Hill Gothic library and chapel and a collection of teapots, musical boxes and visiting-card cases assembled by its owner, Majorie Mockler.

Ashbury

Ashdown House (N.T.) 1D

Open: *Woodlands: Sat–Thur, dawn to dusk all year. Hall, Stairway, Roof and Grounds only: Apr–Oct, Wed, Sat 2–6 (closed Easter and B.H. Mon). Tours at 2.15, 3.15, 4.15 and 5.15.*
Three miles north-west of Lambourn and just into Oxfordshire, Ashdown is an unusual 17th-C. house built by the

first Lord Craven for Elizabeth of Bohemia. It has a magnificent staircase and roof crowned by a cupola and golden ball.

Banbury

Banbury is probably best known for two things – the famous cross mentioned in the nursery rhyme and the currant-filled cakes. Both are still happily in evidence in this large market town, though the cross we see today is a 19th-C. replacement, as the original was destroyed by the Puritans, along with Banbury Castle.

Banbury Museum 2A

Open: *Apr–Sept, Mon–Sat and B.H. Mon 10–5; Oct–Mar, Tue–Sat 10–4.30. Closed Good Fri, Christmas, Boxing Day and New Year's Day. Tel: Banbury (0295) 259855.*

In a restored Edwardian building by the Banbury Cross, the museum emphasises the history of the town and Cherwell Valley. An attractive bookshop and coffee bar share quarters with the Tourist Information Centre.

Morland and Company

carries on a brewing tradition of over 250 years. In 1711 John Morland, a local farmer, purchased a West Ilsley property with a malthouse. Soon a brewhouse was added and the company has grown steadily since that time. Today it serves over 200 licensed houses and many free-trade houses in several counties. Their products include a variety of draught and bottled beers, including Old Speckled Hen, Revival Dark Mild, 1711 Bitter, Old Masters and the Monarch range of ales. *Tel: Abingdon (0235) 553377.*

Mary Holland Ltd

organises craft and antique fairs, often in distinguished surroundings. *Tel: Abingdon (0235) 21873.*

Broughton Castle

Bloxham Village Museum 2A

Open: *Easter–Sept, Sun, B.H. Mon 2.30–5.30; Oct, Sun 2.30–4.30; Nov–Easter 2nd Sun in each month 2.30–4.30. Tel: Banbury (0295) 720283.*
Located in the Old Court House in Church Street, the museum's 1990 exhibits will be Bloxham in Photographs and Bloxham Schools.

Broughton Castle 2A

Open: *17 May–12 Sept, Wed, Sun and B.H. Mon; also Thur in July, Aug. and Easter B.H. Mon. Tel: Banbury (0295) 262624/812027.*
Just two miles from Banbury is Broughton Castle, mainly an Elizabethan building, standing in parkland like a fairy-tale castle surrounded by a broad moat. Originally built in 1306, it has been the family home of the Fiennes family, Lord Saye and Sele, for the last 600 years. The Elizabethan front and fireplaces, ceilings and panelling were added between 1554 and 1559. There

are interesting Civil War connections, the 8th Lord Saye and Sele having been a distinguished member of the Parliamentary Party.

A Day in the Country

Upper Aynho Grounds, Aynho, near Banbury. Tel: (0869) 345210.
A Day in the Country offers a chance to be a country squire for a day with clay pigeon shooting, fly fishing and cordon bleu food served in a cosy 17th-C. barn converted to a conference and exhibition area. Company entertainment with a difference.

Wendy Fair Markets

organises large Sunday markets in all parts of the country. Finmere in Oxfordshire and Bovingdon in Hertfordshire are among their main venues. *Tel: Ruislip (0895) 675558.*

Burford

Surely one of the most beautiful of all English small towns, Burford contains a delightful and harmonious mixture of stone buildings. The sweep of the graceful High Street down to the little bridge over the Windrush is one of the Cotswolds' most stunning sights.

Burford Garden Centre 1C

Open: *Mar–Oct, Mon–Fri 9–5.30, Sat–Sun 9.30–5.45; Nov–Feb, Mon–Fri 9–5.15, Sat–Sun 9.30–5. Closed Christmas Day. Tel: Burford (099382) 3117.*
On the southern edge of the town, just south of the A40, is Burford Garden Centre, which also contains a working craft centre, adventure playground and a coffee shop.

Cotswold Wild Life Park 1C

Open: *daily 10–6 (or dusk). Tel: Burford (099382) 3006.*
South of Burford in an attractive wooded estate is the Cotswold Wild Life Park. Here many species of wildlife roam in the open,

66

separated from visitors by ditches so as not to spoil the uninterrupted views. Leopard, white rhino, zebra, ostrich and the famous hide-and-seek red panda are just some of the animal attractions. There is also a butterfly house, aquarium, narrow-gauge railway and adventure playground to add to the fun.

Cotswold Woollen Weavers 1C

Open: *Mon–Sat 10–6, Sun 2–6.* *Coaches by appointment only.* *Tel: Filkins (036786) 491.*
Five hundred years ago great flocks of sheep roamed the Cotswold Hills. Nowadays there are fewer sheep, but in the delightful village of Filkins, between Burford and Lechlade, some of the old ways live on. Cotswold Woollen Weavers uses traditional skills and machinery to manufacture a wide range of Woolmark cloth, garments, knitwear, rugs and accessories. You can tour the working mill and exhibition areas and browse in the well-stocked mill shop. There's a coffee shop (with newspapers) and picnic area too.

Didcot Railway Centre

Cotswold Wild Life Park

Maidaid Thames and Chilterns Ltd offers a range of glass-washing appliances for use in pubs, hotels and restaurants. *Tel: Middleton Stoney (086 989) 460/485.*

Tolsey Museum 1C

Open: *Easter–Oct, daily 2–5.30.* *Tel: Clanfield (036781) 294.*
Burford's history is celebrated at the Tolsey Museum in the High Street, which contains maces, seals and history of coopering and rope-making.

Charlbury

Charlbury stands in the Evenlode Valley close to the Wychwood Forest, and was first mentioned in the 7th-C. as the burial place of St Diuma, first Bishop of Lichfield.

Charlbury Museum 1B

Key from the pharmacy opposite, upon payment of 30p. Open: Apr–Oct, Sun 2–4.
Charlbury Museum in Market Street contains a small collection of local photographs and articles of domestic and industrial use.

Chipping Norton 1B

Chipping Norton, situated between Oxford and Stratford, is a favourite stopping-off point for visitors. Standing some 650 feet up in the Cotswolds, it is the highest town in Oxfordshire.

Near the attractive villages of Great and Little Rollright are the remarkable Rollright Stones, a late Neolithic stone circle. The circle contains seventy stones including the 'King' stone and the four 'Whispering Knights' and is thought to have been constructed around 1500 BC. Memorable views.

Didcot
Didcot Railway Centre 2C

Open: *Apr–Sept, Tue–Sun and B.H. Mon 11–5; Oct–Mar, Sat, Sun 11–5 (dusk in winter). Tel: Didcot (0235) 817200.*
Reflecting its industrial heritage, Didcot has a fine railway centre, established by the Great Western Society as a working museum. Here, alongside Brunel's main line to the west is a large collection of former GWR locomotives, coaches and rolling-stock of all kinds, covering 100 years of railway history. The original engine shed, coaling stage, turntable and lifting-shop, as well as a re-created station of the times, are great attractions. On special steaming days locomotives are in steam and rides are given.

Dorchester

Dorchester Abbey Museum 2C

Open: *Good Fri, Easter Sat–Mon, 21, 22, 28, 29 Apr; May–Sept, Tue–Sat 10.30–12.30 and 2–6; also 6, 7, 13, 14 Oct and B.H. Mons. Tel: Oxford (0865) 340056.*

Dorchester's superb medieval abbey church dominates this delightful village with its timbered houses, thatched cottages, ancient inns and inviting shops.

Around the village are some pleasant walks, some of which take you past the remains of Dorchester's earlier settlements. A small museum displays artefacts of local history.

Notcutts Garden Centre and Mattock's Roses 2C

Open: *Mon–Sat 9–5; Sun, B.H. Mon (except Christmas and Jan) 10.30–5. Tel: Nuneham Courtenay (086 738) 454.*

Just to the north are a beautifully laid out garden centre, rose gardens and rose fields. Restaurant and toilets (disabled facilities). On B4015 at junction with A423 south of Nuneham Courtenay.

Faringdon

The ancient town of Faringdon has several royal connections: King Alfred had a palace here; his son Edward, first King of England,

Halliday's Antiques

Tel: Oxford (0865) 340028.

Housed in one of Dorchester's magnificent Georgian buildings, Halliday's is one of the largest antiques showrooms in England and specialises in 18th-C. furnishings, fireplaces and panelling. Here you can enjoy looking at exceptionally beautiful antiques in a setting to match.

died here and King John gave the town a royal charter to hold a weekly market in 1218. The market still continues today. Faringdon is a pleasant centre with buildings dating back to the 17th or 18th centuries, some with Civil War associations. At the heart of the market town, where five roads meet, is the Market Hall, supported on stone pillars.

Buscot Park (N.T.) 1C

Opens: *4 Apr–Sept, Wed–Fri, Easter Sat and Sun, 2nd and 4th Sat and Sun in each month, 2–6. Closed B.H. Tel: Faringdon (0367) 20786 weekdays only.*

Astride the A417 near Faringdon is Buscot Park and its fine Adam-style house built in 1780, the home of the Faringdon collection of paintings and furniture. The Park is landscaped with extensive water gardens.

Great Coxwell Barn (N.T.) 1C

Open: *any reasonable time.*

Two miles south between the A420 and B4019 is the Great Coxwell Barn, a remarkable monastic stone barn built by the Cistercians in the 13th C. One of the country's largest tithe barns, it is now preserved by the National Trust.

Henley

Henley-on-Thames is probably best known for its boating connections. It was here that the first Oxford and Cambridge boat race was staged in 1829. Ten years later, Henley Regatta was established. Today Henley Royal Regatta, which takes place the first week of July, is a prestigious occasion attracting crews and visitors from all over the world.

Boat hire or passenger trips are operated from this stretch of the Thames (see Leisure Afloat).

Stonor Park

Henley Regatta

Greys Court (N.T.) 3D

Open: *Apr–Sept, House: Mon, Wed & Fri 2–6; Garden: Mon–Sat 2–6. Closed Good Fri. Tel: Rotherfield Greys (049 17) 529.*
Three miles west of Henley on the A423 is Greys Court, a charming 17th-C. manor house set among the picturesque ruins of the original 13th-C. house. Points of interest include a Tudor well-house with a large donkey wheel set over a remarkable 200-foot well (lit so that you can peer into its depths) and a comparatively recent Archbishop's Maze.

Henley Festival of Music and the Arts

Now in its 8th year, this four-day festival combines the pleasures of music, painting, sculpture, theatre, cabaret and dancing with good food and wine in the elegant riverside setting of the Stewards' Enclosure at the world's most famous regatta. *Tel: Henley (0491) 410414.*

Maharajah's Well 3D

Open: *any reasonable time.*
A few miles west towards Stoke Row on the B481 is the Maharajah's Well. This example of exotica looks like a miniature bandstand from the road, but is in fact a well given by the Maharaja of Benares to Mr E.A. Reade in gratitude for his work on the water supply system in Benares in 1863.

Stonor Park 3D

Open: *Apr–Sept, Sat (Aug only) Sun, Wed (from May 2), Thurs (July and Aug) 2–5.30. B.H. Mons 11–5.30. Tel: Turville Heath (049 163) 587.*
Set in a fold in the beautiful Chiltern Hills five miles north of Henley is the historic home of the

Gunn Communications

is a public relations firm handling press relations, product launches, company newsletters and promotional print. *Tel: Henley (0491) 579600.*

Stonor family. For more than 800 years they have owned the secluded deer park, and parts of the house date from the earliest days of ownership. Throughout the centuries, Stonor has been a centre for Catholicism, and the medieval chapel is still used for the celebration of Mass. An exhibition features the life and work of Sir Edmund Campion, who hid in the house in 1581, prior to his execution. Stonor is still a family home with many items f rare and unusual furniture, numerous family portraits and collections of bronze sculptures, silhouettes and tapestries.

Friars Court Leisure Activities,

on a working farm in Clanfield, conducts knowledgeable guided walks, by appointment, along their conservation farm trail. They also offer restful, riverside camping sites, boating and clay shoots. Cream teas are a speciality. *Tel: Clanfield (036781) 206.*

69

Kingston Bagpuize

Kingston House 2C
Open: May, June, Sept, Sun, Wed; B.H. Mon in May, August; 2.30–5.30. Tel: Longworth (0865) 820259.
Kingston House is a superb Charles II manor house with a magnificent cantilevered staircase and well-proportioned panelled rooms with fine furniture and pictures. The large garden contains many interesting flowering shrubs and bulbs, as well as a woodland garden, herbaceous borders and some fine trees.

Millets Farm 2C
Open: daily 9–6. Tel: Frilford Heath (0865) 391555 for recorded information.
Two miles east on the A415 near Frilford is a large, pick-your-own fruit and vegetable farm. There is also a newly remodeled farm shop, an attractive garden centre, a pets corner, trout fishery and picnic area. The Munchery serves tasty snacks and light meals.

Mapledurham

Mapledurham House 3D
Open: Easter–Sept, Sat, Sun, B.H. Mon 2.30–5. Tel: Reading (0734) 723350.

Mapledurham Watermill 3D
Open: Easter–Oct, Sat, Sun, B.H. Mon 1–5, Jan–Easter, Sun 2–4. Tel: Reading (0734) 723350.
Beside the Thames on the Oxfordshire/Berkshire border just west of Reading are the Elizabethan mansion and watermill of Mapledurham. Ideally you should try to visit this charming olde-worlde village by boat from Reading (see Leisure Afloat).
Mapledurham House, with its paintings, moulded plasterwork and beautiful family chapel, is the centrepiece of the village. There is a riverside picnic park. At the restored watermill you can see into the mechanism as wheat is ground with original machinery and mill stones.

70

Oxford Association of Hotels and Guest Houses
Tel: Oxford (0865) 722995.
The association has 75 members in the city, providing a good standard of accommodation at prices from £12 per person per night upwards.

Oxford
Oxford is a remarkable and beautiful city, and home of the most famous seat of learning in the world. There is so much to see that it is impossible to do the city justice in a few hours or even a few days of sightseeing.
It is a city of architectural splendours with more than 600 listed buildings in the centre square mile alone. Its museums and art galleries are some of the finest and most exciting in Britain and it has one of the largest libraries in the world. Two lovely rivers, the Thames and the Cherwell, grace the city, and there are many gardens, meadows and parks.

Colleges
Most colleges open their quadrangles and chapels to visitors in the afternoon. Full details of opening times are given in *Welcome to Oxford*, available from Oxford Information Centre or the Thames and Chilterns Tourist Board.

Mapledurham House

Ashmolean Museum 2C
Open: Tue–Sat 10–4, Sun 2–4, Summer B.H. Mon 2–5. Closed Good Fri, Easter Sat, Sun and Sept during St Giles Fair. Tel: Oxford (0865) 278000.
The Ashmolean Museum in Beaumont Street was founded by Elias Ashmole in 1683, sixty years before the British Museum. It is Britain's oldest public museum, now housed in a lovely classical building of the 1840s, and contains the University's outstanding and priceless collections. Among them is a major collection of Michaelangelo drawings; Pre-Raphaelite and French impressionist works; European silver; British antiquities including the celebrated 9th-C. Alfred Jewel and one of the finest treasures of Egyptian, Greek and Roman antiquities.

B.H. Blackwell's, the
famous bookshop, is one of the great institutions of Oxford. There are actually six bookshops in the centre of Oxford specialising in children's books, paperbacks, art and music as well, as the main bookshop in Broad Street. Tel: Oxford (0865) 249111.

Bate Collection of Historical Instruments 2C
Faculty of Music, St Aldate's Open: Mon–Fri 2–5. Tel: Oxford (0865) 276139.

PHONE 'TOURISTLINE'

Oxford (0865) 244888
24-hour recorded details
of what to see and do
in and around Oxford.

Bodleian Library 2C

Open: *Divinity School and
Exhibition Room: Mon–Fri 9–5,
Sat 9–12.30. Guided Tours of the
Divinity School, Convocation
House and Duke Humfrey's
Library: Apr–Sept, Mon–Fri at
10.30, 11.30, 2 and 3; Sat 10.30,
11.30. Please note no children
under 14 are admitted. Tel:
Oxford (0865) 277000.*
The Bodleian in Broad Street is
one of the world's greatest
libraries. It was first established in
1602 and today has some five
million books.
   The Divinity School was built
between 1420 and 1490 and is
noted for its exquisite fan vaulting.

Botanic Garden 2C

High Street
Open: *daily 9–5 (4.30 in winter).
Glasshouses daily 2–4. Closed
Good Fri and Christmas Day. Tel:
Oxford (0865) 276920/276921.*
A collection of over 8000 species
of plants in the garden and
greenhouses. Collections of
carnivorous plants, tropical water
lilies, roses and variegated plants
plus herbaceous borders, and bog
and rock gardens.

Carfax Tower 2C

Open: *27 Mar–Oct, Mon–Sat
10–6, Sun 2–6. Last entry 5.45.
Tel: Oxford (0865) 250239.*
In the heart of the city, the tower is
all that remains of the 14th-C. city
church of St Martin, demolished
to widen the roadway. Note the
clock on the east side with the
'Quarter Boys' chiming every
quarter hour. Superb views from
the top.

Divinity School, Bodleian Library

Christ Church 2C

Open: *May–Sept, Mon–Sat
9.30–6, Sun 12.30–4.30; Oct–
Apr, Mon–Sat 9.30–4.30, Sun
12.30–4.30. Tel: Oxford (0865)
276154. Picture Gallery (own
entrance from Oriel Square):
Mon–Sat 10.30–1, 2–5.30, Sun
2–5.30 (Oct–Easter closes at
4.30 and closed for one week at
Christmas and Easter). Tel:
Oxford (0865) 276172.*
One of the largest colleges, Christ
Church was founded in 1546 by
Henry VIII. Its majestic sights
include Tom Quad (Oxford's
largest), Tom Tower (designed by
Wren) and the magnificent
cathedral hall. The picture gallery,
of modern design, houses a fine
collection of Old Masters.

Church of St Michael at the North Gate 2C

Open: *Mon–Sat 10–5, Sun
12.30–5 (closes at 4 in winter
and during services). Tel: Oxford
(0865) 240940.*
The Saxon tower of the church of
St Michael at the North Gate in
Cornmarket Street dates from the
first half of the 11th C. and is
Oxford's oldest building. The
church treasury displays rare silver
and documents and you can
examine the mechanism and bells
of the church clock.

Language Schools

As a world-famous centre of learning, Oxford attracts
students of many kinds, including those who come to the
city to improve their English and those learning business and
secretarial skills.

Brown and Brown Oxford Tutorial College, *South Suite,
Frewin Court, off Cornmarket. Tel: Oxford (0865) 728280.*

Eckersley School of English, *14 Friars Entry. Tel: Oxford
(0865) 721268.*

Executive School, *8 Market Place, Abingdon, Oxon. Tel:
Abingdon (0235) 554747.*

Godmer House School of English, *90 Banbury Road, Tel:
Oxford (0865) 515566.*

Lake School of English Ltd, *14b Park End Street, Tel: Oxford
(0865) 724312.*

Oxford House School of English, *i67 High Street,
Wheatley, near Oxford. Tel: Wheatley (08677) 4786.*

Oxford Study Centre, *17 Sunderland Avenue. Tel: Abingdon
(0235) 554747.*

Swan School of English, *111 Banbury Road. Tel: Oxford
(0865) 53201.*

UTS Oxford Centre, *2 Gloucester Street (after 1 May, 66
Banbury Road). Tel: Oxford (0865) 726745.*

The Temple Club, in the
Oxford Road, Cowley, is a
smart sports and nightclub
with a restaurant/function
room. *Tel: Oxford (0865)
779115.*

Britain in Bloom

Every year a country-wide competition is held to find Britain's most florally attractive cities, towns and villages. In 1989, for the third consecutive year, Oxford was judged a joint winner in this prestgious event, officially making it one of Britain's two most beautiful large cities.

Many towns and villages in the Thames and Chilterns compete, and at the Regional level, Dorchester-on-Thames, Eton and Banbury were again winners in the large village, small town and large town divisions, respectively.

Ice Rink 2C
Oxpens Road
Open: daily. Tel: Oxford (0865) 247676.

Museum of the History of Science 2C
Broad Street
Open: Mon–Fri 10.30–1, 2.30–4. Tel: Oxford (0865) 277280.

Museum of Modern Art 2C
Open: Tue–Sat 10–6, Sun 2–6. Tel: Oxford (0865) 722733.
The Museum of Modern Art in Pembroke Street has a bookshop and coffee bar, and excellent

Corpus Christi College

facilities for the disabled. This lively gallery features frequently changing exhibitions by leading international contemporary artists. Educational activities, films, workshops and seminars accompany each exhibition. Full details are available from a regularly published news-sheet

J.D. Barclay of Barclay House, Botley Road, Oxford, specialises in self-drive car, van and mini-bus hire. Tel: Oxford (0865) 722444.

Brize Self Drive offers a fully inclusive small-car rate of £94 per week. Tel: daytime, Witney (0993) 775126; evening, Shipton under Wychwood (0993) 831378.

Luxride Hire, 14 Milestone Road, Carterton, provides a licenced taxi and private hire service. Tel: Carterton (0993) 841480.

Oxford Bus Co. operates bus services in Oxford and the surrounding area, as well as a fast CityLink service to London, and Heathrow and Gatwick. Tel: General enquiries, Oxford (0865) 711312; recorded information for 190 Oxford–London service, (0865) 248190, and the X70 Heathrow–Gatwick service, (0865) 722270.

Percivals Coaches (a division of Jeffs Coaches) in Lamarsh Road, Botley, Oxford, hires standard and executive coaches for private British and European travel. Tel: Oxford (0865) 246509.

and the 24-hour telephone enquiry number Oxford (0865) 728608.

Museum of Oxford 2C
St Aldate's
Open: Tue–Sat 10–5. Closed Good Fri, Christmas and Boxing Day. Tel: Oxford (0865) 815559.
This well-kept museum depicts the history of Oxford with graphics, models and reconstructed period rooms.

The Oxford Story 2C
Open: Apr–Oct 9.30–5, Nov–Mar 10–4, daily. (Last admission ½ hour before closing.) Closed Christmas Day. Tel: Oxford (0865) 728822.
In Broad Street is an exciting recent attraction, The Oxford Story. Travel back through time, experiencing eight centuries of the sights, sounds and personalities of Oxford. The Oxford Story blends scholarship and modern audio-visual techniques to bring the University's past to life. Commentary by Sir Alec Guinness.

The City of Oxford Orchestra presents a variety of concerts year round. In summer the 'Beautiful Music in Beautiful Places' series is held in some of Oxford's loveliest college buildings. There are also autumn and spring series featuring distinguished artists. *Tickets from the Orchestra, Tel: Oxford (0865) 240358, and from Blackwell's Music Shop and Tickets in Oxford.*

Music at Oxford presents professional concerts throughout the year in some of Oxford's most distinguished venues. Summer brings the annual Handel in Oxford Festival (1–12 July) and the Grand Fireworks Concerts. There is also an excellent children's series. *Tickets from Music at Oxford, Tel: Oxford (0865) 864056, and from Blackwell's Music Shop and Tickets in Oxford.*

Art in Oxford offers two 2-week residential art courses at Magdalen College, Oxford, during July. The programme emphasises drawing and painting with classes, lectures and field trips. *Tel: Oxford (0865) 56788.*

Arts Council Touring promotes the arts and visits of touring companies in the Oxford area. *Tel: Oxford (0865) 727179.*

Banquets of Oxford provides high-quality catering services. *Tel: Oxford (0865) 59961.*

Morrells Brewery was founded in 1782 by Mark and James Morrell and is thought to be the only independent family-run brewery with a history of more than 200 years of continuing production on the original site. From this fine heritage comes a range of popular beers. The brewery has 136 public houses, all within a 40-mile radius of Oxford. Many are to be found in the city itself; the rest are mainly in the towns and villages of Oxfordshire. *Tel: Oxford (0865) 792013.*

Pitt Rivers Museum 2C
(entrance through University Museum), Parks Road
Open: Mon–Sat 1–4.30. Balfour Building (music gallery): Mon–Sat 1–4.30. Tel: Oxford (0865) 270927.
Ethnography and prehistory from around the world and the Balfour Building's world-wide collection of musical instruments.

Sheldonian Theatre 2C
Open: Mon–Sat 10–12.45, 2–4.45. Closes at 3.45 16 Nov–14 Feb. Tel: Oxford (0865) 277299.
The Sheldonian Theatre in Broad Street is a large assembly hall where many University ceremonies take place, including the granting of degrees. It was built in 1663 and is one of the earliest and best works of Sir Christopher Wren.

University Museum 2C
Parks Road
Open: Mon–Sat 12–5. Closed 1, 2 Jan, 5–7 Apr, 22–31 Dec. Tel: Oxford (0865) 272950.
The University's treasure trove of natural history in a soaring Victorian-Gothic building.

Worcester College 2C
Open: 2–daily, also 9–12 during vacations. Tel: Oxford (0865) 278300.
The mainly 18th-C. buildings and gatehouse of the college dominate the view along Beaumont Street.

The Gallery at Gloucester Green is Oxford's newest shopping complex. In beautifully designed buildings set around the market square, the Gallery houses a mix of specialised shops, restaurants and cafés.

Oxford Antiques Centre
Open: Tue–Sat 10–5. Tel: Oxford (0865) 251075.
Opposite the railway station, in Park End Street, is the Oxford Antiques Centre. Here, in a turn-of-the-century marmalade factory, antiques dealers sell all manner of objects from water-colours and small collectables to 1930s silk dresses. Refreshments at the Marmalade Cat coffee shop.

Alice's Shop
Tel: Oxford (0865) 723793.
A gift shop with a fascinating history is Alice's Shop at 83 St Aldate's. It was here that the real Alice, of Lewis Carroll's *Adventures in Wonderland*, used to come to buy her sweets, and Carroll wove the shop into the story.

Stained Glass Activities
Tel: Tel: Oxford (0865) 727529.
If you've an artistic bent, you may like to book a course in stained glass techniques tutored by Paul San Casciani, Oxford's stained glass artist, or attend one of his 'Come and Make' one-day schools, where you can create a traditional leaded panel or a copperfoil-technique terrarium.

Some well-preserved buildings in the quadrangle date from the 13th and 14th centuries. But it is for the college gardens that Worcester is known. With their large lake, spreading lawns and stately trees they rival the Botanic Gardens for beauty.

Minstrel House, an inviting gift shop selling a wide range of goods has branches at Abingdon and Woodstock and Witney. *Tel: Abingdon (0235) 25605; Woodstock (0993) 812128; Witney (0993) 774216 and 779783.*

The Oxford Collection at 2 Golden Cross, off Cornmarket, is a tasteful gift shop featuring an array of items based on Oxford themes and designs. *Tel: Oxford (0865) 247414.*

Oxford Craft Centre
Covered Market.
Open: *Mon–Sat 9–5.30. Tel: Oxford (0865) 790031.*
Beautiful objects produced by Oxfordshire artists and craftsmen.

Past Times in Turl Street offers a fascinating range of historical replicas and gift items, grouped chronologically. *Tel: Oxford (0865) 791553.*

Scots Corner at 14 Turl Street carries a wide variety of quality Scottish knitwear, tweeds and tartans. *Tel: Oxford (0865) 248342.*

Phillips in Oxford at 39 Park End Street are valuers and auctioneers of fine art, with 20 salesrooms throughout the U.K. *Tel: Oxford (0865) 723524.*

Robbins Theatrical Costumiers Ltd will allow you to become anyone you desire, with the help of their astonishing array of theatrical costumes. *Tel: Oxford (0865) 240268/735524.*

Halls Oxford & West Brewery Company can trace its name back to 1795 when William Hall purchased Swan's Nest Brewery from Sir John Treacher, then Mayor of Oxford.

Today the company runs some 300 pubs in an area stretching from Milton Keynes to Plymouth. Their style varies from traditional hostelry to sophisticated cocktail bar, but all have one thing in common – a welcoming hospitality. *Tel: Oxford (0865) 882255.*

Sonning Common

The Herb Farm 3D
Open: *Tue–Sun 10–5, also B.H. and Christmas. Tel: Reading (0734) 724220.*
Visit the Herb Farm at Sonning Common to see a large range of herbal products in a fine 18th-C. barn. In the display garden (including a formal Knot Garden and a Medieval Garden) are over 200 varieties of culinary, medicinal and aromatic herb plants, all of which are for sale. There's also an interesting collection of antique farm machinery.

Rycote Chapel

Frank Cooper Shop and Museum of Marmalade
Open: *Mon–Sat 10–6; mid May–mid Sept also Sun 12–5. Tel: Oxford (0865) 245125.*
Frank Cooper first started selling his wife's excellent marmalade from his shop at 84 High Street in 1874. Today, you can still find Frank Cooper's Shop and Museum of Marmalade at the original premises.

Stanton Harcourt

The Manor House 2C
Open: *Apr 15, 16, 26, 28; May 3, 6, 7, 17, 20, 24, 27, 28; June 7, 10, 21, 24; July 5, 8, 19, 22; Aug 3, 5, 23, 26, 27; Sept 6, 9, 20, 23, 2–6 each day. Tel: Oxford (0865) 881928.*
Nine miles west of Oxford lie the unique medieval buildings of Stanton Harcourt Manor. Its attractions include the Old Kitchen (one of the few medieval kitchens to survive in England), the charming Domestic Chapel and Pope's Tower, where Alexander Pope completed his translation of Homer's *Iliad* in 1718.

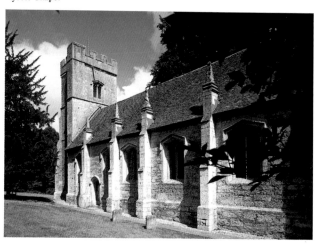

Steeple Aston

Rousham House 2B

Open: *Garden: daily 10–4.30; House: Apr–Sept, Wed, Sun, B.H. Mon 2–4.30. Tel: Steeple Aston (0869) 47110. Please note that children under the age of 15 are not admitted.*

South of Steeple Aston is Rousham House, built in 1635 by Sir Robert Dormer, a Royalist in the Civil War. During eight reigns, court artists and architects were employed to embellish Rousham. It stands in 30 acres of landscaped grounds with cascades, statues, decorative ponds and vistas. Originally designed by William Kent and now his only surviving unaltered landscaped garden, the grounds lie peacefully alongside a beautiful reach of the River Cherwell.

Thame

Thame has been a prosperous market town since before the Norman Conquest. This historic importance is reflected in the great length and breadth of the High Street and in the number of ancient houses and shops that line many of the streets. Thame is also noted for its many old inns, including the Bird Cage in Cornmarket and the restored Spread Eagle, which gained notoriety in the 1920s when the owner, John Fothergill, wrote *An Inn Keeper's Diary.*

Rycote Chapel (E.H.) 3C

Open: *13 Apr–Sept, daily 10–6; Oct–12 Apr, Tue–Sun 10–4. Closed Boxing Day and New Year's Day. Tel: Ickford (08447) 346.*

At Milton Common, three miles south-west of Thame, is Rycote Chapel, the only surviving part of the mansion where Sir Henry Norreys entertained Elizabeth I. This outstanding 15th-C. chapel has medieval stalls, some fine 17th-C. pews and a late 17th-C. ornamental screen. On the ceiling are traces of tiny stars, painted on the back of Elizabethan playing cards.

Uffington 1D

Towering almost 900 feet above Uffington is the celebrated White Horse Hill with its mysterious equine hill figure.

Above the horse is Uffington Castle, an ancient hill fort. Below is Dragon Hill, another place surrounded by legend – some say that this is where St George slew his dragon.

The village of **Ashbury**, three miles south-west, is also the location of another ancient monument, Wayland's Smithy, a prehistoric burial place consisting of a long earthen mound containing a chamber made of large blocks of stone. The legend

The Dovecote, Rousham Park

is that any horse left tethered at the entrance will be shod by Wayland, smith of the Saxon gods, if a coin is left as a fee on the lintel.

Wallingford

The Thames-side market town of Wallingford was already important in Saxon times. In 1067 William the Conqueror used it as a convenient crossing point on the Thames as he sought to subjugate southern England. In 1155 the town received its first charter, making it one of the oldest royal boroughs in the country. Today, a superb 900-foot bridge spans the Thames.

Wallingford Castle 3D

Open: *Grounds: Mar–Oct, daily 10–6.*
Just off Castle Street are the remains of a medieval motte and bailey castle. There are lovely gardens and this is a fine spot for a picnic. An explanatory guidebook is available from the nearby town museum.

Wallingford Museum 3D

Open: *Tue–Fri, B.H. Mon 2–5, Sat 10.30–12.30, 2–5; Jun–Aug, Sun 2–5. Tel: Wallingford (0491) 35065.*
This local museum on the High Street maintains a permanent collection of local history and presents two special exhibits each year.

Wellplace Zoo 3D

Open: *Easter–Sept, daily 10–5.30; Oct–Easter weekends, weather permitting. Tel: Checkendon (0491) 680473/680092.*
South-east of Wallingford off the A407 at Ipsden is the 6½-acre Wellplace Zoo for children. There is a large collection of animals, some of which can be petted and fed. A cafeteria, play area and picnic area complete the picture.

Cholsey Railway 3D

Open: *Station: Jan–Dec, first Sun in each month. Trains: Apr–1 Oct, first and last Suns in each month and B.H. Mons. Tel: Wallingford (0491) 35067 (weekends).*

From the Cholsey and Wallingford Industrial Estate south of the town, this railway runs on a preserved Great Western Railway branch line towards Cholsey. There is a museum and souvenir shop and snacks are available. Ample parking.

Wantage

Wantage's most famous son is undoubtedly King Alfred the Great, who was born there in AD 849 and whose statue now dominates the Market Place. There are a number of period houses of note in Wantage, mainly built of mellowed red and local blue-glazed bricks. Stile's Almshouses, founded in the 17th C., are notable for having an entrance cobbled with sheep's knucklebones.

Ardington Pottery

Ardington Pottery 2D

Open: *Mon–Sat 10–5, Sun 2–5. Tel: Abingdon (0235) 833302.*
Between Wantage and the village of East Hendred lies the estate village of Ardington, where Home Farm provides a cluster of workshops for a group of craftsmen, including potters Les and Brenda Owens.

The Owens' workshop is the perfect example of a 19th-C. dairy. Look for the hand-painted ceramic picture tiles and marble benches which have been retained in the old butter room.

Kingstone Lisle Park 1D

Open: *Easter–Sept, Thur and B.H. (Sat, Sun, Mon) 2–5. Tel: Uffington (036782) 223.*
At Kingstone Lisle, 4 miles west of Wantage, is the famous Blowing Stone, a large perforated sarsen stone which produces a fog-horn-like sound when blown. Local tradition associates it with King Alfred. In the village stands Kingstone Lisle Park, a mainly early 19th-C. house with a dramatic flying staircase, fine furnishings and attractive gardens.

Vale and Downland Museum Centre 2D

Open: *Tue–Sat 10.30–4.30, Sun 2.30–5. Open some B.H. Mon, closed from Christmas through New Year's Day. Tel: Wantage (02357) 66838.*
This most attractive local museum in Church Street tells the story of Wantage and the surrounding area over the centuries. Museum shop and pleasing café.

Venn Mill 2C

Open: *2nd Sun in month Apr–Oct, 10–5. Tel: Stanford-in-the-Vale (03677) 8888.*
On the A338 Wantage to Oxford road at Garford is a watermill dating from about 1800 but built on an ancient site. Venn Mill is being carefully restored and will eventually be in full working condition.

Wheatley

Waterperry Gardens 3C

Open: *daily from 10. Tel: Ickford (08447) 226/254. 'Art in Action' 1990, 19–22 July.*
These spacious and peaceful ornamental gardens covering six acres are set in the 83-acre estate of the 18th-C. Waterperry House

(not usually open to the public). For year-round interest there are plants and fine trees, lawns, borders and a riverside walk, together with the herbaceous, alpine and shrub nurseries, and a fruit farm which provide plants and produce for sale at the Garden Shop. There is a Saxon village church in the grounds and homemade refreshments are available in the teashop. Each July the Gardens host a splendid tented four-day craft fair, 'Art in Action'.

Witney

Cogges Manor Farm Museum 1C

Open: *2 Apr–4 Nov 10.30–5.30. Tel: Witney (0993) 772602.*
On the edge of Witney is a 19-acre Edwardian farm museum run by Oxfordshire's Department of Leisure and Arts. Inside the manor-house, in the dairy and in the stables, sheds and barns you'll find agricultural life recreated as it was at the turn of the century. Regular demonstrations of blacksmithing, hurdle making, sheep shearing, butter churning, hand milking, farmhouse cooking and many other skills throughout the season. Horses, cattle, sheep, pigs and poultry typical of the period can be seen, and nature and history trails take the visitor around the site and down to the River Windrush. You can picnic in the sheltered orchard or eat in the cafeteria of the Visitors' Centre, carefully restored from an old milking shed.

Minster Lovell Hall (E.H.) 1C

Open: *13 Apr–Sept, daily 10–6; Oct–12 Apr, Tue–Sun 10–4. Closed 1 Jan and 24–26 Dec. Tel: Witney (0993) 775315.*
On the banks of the River Windrush stand the impressive ruins of Minster Lovell Hall. A dovecote, the almost untouched 15th-C. church, and the romantic

Waterperry Gardens

ruins make this an especially beautiful Oxfordshire scene. Local lore has it that a skeleton found in the 18th C. was that of Lord Lovell.

North Leigh Roman Villa (E.H.) 2B

Open: *13 Apr–Sept, daily 10–6. Tel: Witney (0993) 881830.*
There was a settlement at North Leigh, three miles north-east, even before Roman times. Visitors today can see evidence of those early inhabitants at the earthworks known as Grim's Dyke. The courtyard villa had more than 60 rooms. There is a fine mosaic on view.

Cogges Manor Farm Museum

Woodstock

Though the elegant town of Woodstock presents a mainly Georgian façade to the world, some 16th- and 17th-C. traces can still be seen, and behind many a Victorian frontage are earlier beamed and panelled interiors. The history of the town goes back to Henry I, who created it to house those he evicted from their land by enclosing a hunting preserve.

It is famous for its glove-making industry, which still continues today in Chaucer Lane.

There are also many charming shops to appeal to visitors, including antique, gift and specialist clothing shops.

Blenheim Palace

Blenheim Palace 2B

Open: *Park: daily 9–5; Palace: 12 Mar–Oct, daily 10.30–5.30 (last admission 4.45); Garden Centre: mid Mar–Oct, daily 10–6, Nov–mid Mar, daily 10.30–4.30; Butterfly House: mid Mar–Oct, daily 10–6. Tel: Woodstock (0993) 811325.*

Blenheim Palace, the country's largest private house, is perhaps best known as the birthplace of Sir Winston Churchill. This splendid classical mansion, a masterpiece of Sir John Vanbrugh, was a gift from Queen Anne on behalf of a 'grateful nation' to the first Duke of Marlborough after his victory over the French and Bavarians at Blenheim in 1704. Today it is the home of the 11th Duke of Marlborough. It contains a fine collection of furniture, pictures and tapestries, as well as an exhibition of Churchill memorabilia. The simple room where Churchill was born and some of his paintings are also on display.

The 2,000-acre gardens at Blenheim are as splendid as the house and were landscaped in the late 18th C. by 'Capability' Brown. Family attractions at Blenheim include a Butterfly House and an Adventure Playground.

Mosaic at North Leigh Roman Villa (see p. 77)

Combe Mill 2B

Open: *20 May, 26, 27 Aug, 21 Oct 10–5. Tel: Kidlington (08675) 2652.*
At the Blenheim Estates sawmill on the River Evenlode is Combe Mill, where an original beam engine of 1852 has been lovingly restored by a group of enthusiasts who put it in steam and get it to work on many weekends through the summer.

Oxfordshire County Museum 2B

Open: *May–Sept, Mon–Fri 10–5, Sat 10–6, Sun 2–6; Oct–Apr, Tue–Fri 10–4, Sat 10–5, Sun 2–5. Tel: Woodstock (0993) 811456.*
Woodstock's centre extends from the marketplace to the main gates of Blenheim Palace. The 16th-C. Fletchers House in Park Street houses the County Museum, which traces Oxfordshire's development from Neolithic times to the present day. Outside is a curious set of stocks with five leg holes.

Leisure Afloat

Though far from the sea, you're never very far from water in the Thames and Chilterns. It is an area crossed by some of our greatest waterways, notably the Grand Union, Oxford, and Kennet and Avon Canals, the Lee and Stort Navigation, the Great Ouse and the Thames. You can travel the quiet canals through breathtaking scenery in a traditional narrowboat, or explore unspoilt riverside corners in craft ranging from the humble punt to a luxury cruiser.

The operators listed below are members of the Thames and Chilterns Tourist Board. The map reference following each name refers to the relevant county map.

Oxford Cruisers on the Thames

Grand Union Canal

Arcturus, (2C) Cassio Wharf, Watford, Herts. Tel: Welwyn (043871) 4528.
Passenger trips and private charter aboard narrow boat 'Arcturus', built in 1934.

Bridgewater Boats (1B) Castle Wharf, Berkhamsted, Herts. Tel: Berkhamsted (0442) 863615.
Lovingly cared-for holiday canal boats for exploring miles of regional waterways.

English Waterway Cruises (1C) Bossington Wharf, Rothschild Road, Linslade, Leighton Buzzard, Beds. Tel: Leighton Buzzard (0525) 850184.
Hotel-boat cruises along England's canals and waterways.

Grebe Canal Cruises (2B) Pitstone Wharf, Pitstone, near Ivinghoe, Bucks. Tel: Cheddington (0296) 661920.
Narrow boats for holiday hire, charter and passenger cruises along the Canal.

Kennet and Avon Canal

Kennet Horse Boat Company (2B) 32 West Mills, Newbury, Berks, Tel: Newbury (0635) 44154.
Passenger trips and private charter in traditional motor and horse-drawn barges.

High Line Yachting (3D) Mansion Lane, Iver, Bucks. Tel: Iver (0753) 651496.
Two- to eight-berth narrow boat charter covering the South.

Leighton Lady Cruises (2B) 2 Canal Side, Leighton Buzzard, Beds. Tel: Leighton Buzzard (0525) 384563.
Party cruises on the 54-seat 'Leighton Lady' and self-drive day hire.

Linda Cruises (2B) Cosgrove Wharf, Cosgrove, Milton Keynes, Bucks. Tel: Milton Keynes (0908) 563377.
Narrow boat public trips and private charter.

Lee and Stort Navigation

Adventuress Cruises (4B) Unit X, The Maltings, Station Road, Sawbridgeworth, Herts. Tel: (0279) 600848.
Year-round public trips and group charter on fully enclosed 54-seat passenger boat.

River Thames

Abingdon Boat Centre (2C) Nag's Head Island, Abingdon, Oxon. Tel: Abingdon (0235) 21125.
Hire cruisers, day boats and rowing boats.

Boat Enquiries, (2C) 43 Botley Road, Oxford. Tel: Oxford (0865) 727288. *Hire cruisers on the Thames, canals, the Severn and Avon.*

Classic Cruisers (4B) Whytegates House, Berries Road, Cookham, Berks. Tel: Bourne End (06285) 21189. *Restored Edwardian launch for private hire from Boulter's Lock.*

Catamaran Cruisers Ltd, Charing Cross Pier, Victoria Embankment, London. *Passenger trips,* Tel: (01 839) 2349; Private charter from London, Tel: (01 839) 3572.

The Edwardian, Monro House, 40–42 King Street, London. Tel: (01 379) 5042. *Exclusive Edwardian-style steam launch for private hire from London.*

French Brothers and Windsor Boats (4B) The Runnymede Boathouse, Windsor Road, Old Windsor, Berks. Tel: Windsor (0753) 851900/862933. *Public trips and private charter from the Runnymede Boathouse and from the Promenade, Barry Avenue, Central Windsor.*

Hobbs and Sons Ltd (3D) Station Road, Henley, Oxon. Tel: Henley (0491) 572035. *Hire cruisers, passenge trips and private charter from Henley.*

Kris Cruisers (4B) The Waterfront, Southlea Road, Datchet, Berks. Tel: Windsor (0753) 584866/43930. *Rowing boats, hire cruisers and electric Edwardian lady craft.*

Oxford Cruisers (2C) Eynsham, Oxon. Tel: Oxford (0865) 881698. *Hire cruisers and traditional steel narrow boats from the Boat Hire Centre, off the B4044 between Farmoor and Eynsham toll bridge.*

River Days (2D) Bridge Close, Riverside, Marlow, Bucks. Tel: Marlow (06284) 72805. Luxury day cruises on vintage Edwardian launch between Windsor and Shiplake.

Salter Brothers Ltd (2C) Folly Bridge, Oxford. Tel: Oxford (0865) 243421. *Passenger boat operators between Oxford and Abingdon; Reading and Henley; Marlow, Cookham, Maidenhead and Windsor; and Staines and Windsor. Hire cruisers from Oxford and Reading.*

Showboat (4B) Weir Bank, Bray-on-Thames, Berks. Tel: Maidenhead (0628) 770011. *Private hire cruises on a paddle-steamer and a river cruiser from points between Windsor and Henley. Simulated clay pigeon shoot.*

Thames Cruises (1C) 5 Bourton Close, Clanfield, Oxon. Tel: Clanfield (036781) 313. *Passanger trips and private charter on 48-seat narrow boat from historic Radcot Bridge on A4095.*

Thames Rivercruise (3B) Pipers Island, Bridge Street, Caversham Bridge, Reading, Berks. Tel: Reading (0734) 481088. *Private charter and passenger trips, including tours to Mapledurham.*

The Thames Hire Cruiser Association, 19 Acre End Street, Eynsham, Oxford OX8 1PE. Tel: Oxford (0865) 880107. With 20 members and 500 holiday cruisers for hire, the THCA is in a unique position to provide you with just the kind of boat you seek for your River Thames holiday.

The Association was formed to lay down minimum standards for the quality of boats and their equipment and to provide mutual assistance in case of mechanical trouble.

Another benefit is the facility to moor overnight at other members' yards – a boon during the busiest periods of the year.

The Thames at Cliveden

Further Afield

Not all of the Thames and Chilterns Tourist Board's members are to be found in the region. Recognising the value of being a member, several tourist attractions and other organizations outside the Region have decided to join us. Among them you will find some of the country's foremost attractions, as well as some useful, interesting and unusual services.

The nearby county of Wiltshire is the home of **Arkell's Brewery**, owner of 64 pubs in the county, all serving traditional beer. Founded by John Arkell in 1843, the brewery is still family-owned. *Kingsdown Brewery, Stratton St Margaret, Swindon, Wilts. Tel: Swindon (0793) 823026.*

Blackland Lakes Holiday and Leisure Centre at Calne in Wiltshire is an ideal family holiday and leisure centre with a nature reserve, wildfowl collection and coarse fishing. *Tel: Calne (0249) 813672.*

Castle Ashby, off the A428 just into Northants, is a 16th-C. mansion in 200 acres of parkland. The castle is a major venue for events from product launches to conferences. Only the gardens are open to the public, daily, dawn till dusk. *Tel: Yardley Hastings (060 129) 234.*

The well-known brewers **Charrington**, and their associated companies Toby Restaurants and Vintage Inns, operate more than 400 pubs in the Thames and Chilterns area. Many have restaurants and some have letting bedrooms. Some of Britain's finest historic taverns can be found in this part of the country. *Charrington and Co., Anchor House, Mile End, London. Tel: (01 790) 1860.*

Royal Air Force Museum, Hendon (see over)

Chessington World of Adventures, just off the A423 from junction 9 of the M25, offers family fun and excitement. This extensive, one-price theme park will open Europe's first hanging roller coaster in 1990. There are also large zoological gardens and a children's water ride. *Leatherhead Road*, Chessington, Surrey. Tel: Epsom (03727) 27227.

The **Cotswold Farm Park** at Guiting Power near Cheltenham, Glos., contains a comprehensive and delightful collection of rare breeds of British farm animals from little Soay sheep to magnificent long-horn cattle and spotty Gloucester pigs. *Tel: Guiting Power (04515) 307.*

Croft Publications produces numerous free, local eating-out guides from Chapman House, 10 Blackheath Village, London. *Tel: (01 403) 0609.*

Set in a wooded Gloucestershire valley, the **Dean Heritage Centre** reflects the unique character of the Forest of Dean. There is a craft centre, reconstructed cottage and mine, water wheel and an adventure playground, as well as special events and exhibitions throughout the year. *Dean Heritage Centre, Camp Mill, Cinderford, Gloucestershire. Tel: Dean (0594) 22170.*

At the Trocadero in London's Piccadilly Circus you will find the **Guinness World of Records**, an exciting exhibition which transforms the pages of the best-selling book into a three-dimensional experience. *Guinness World of Records, The Trocadero, Piccadilly, London. Tel: (01 439) 7331.*

The scenic **Kennet Country** of neighbouring Wiltshire takes in the western reaches of the

Chiltern Hills. This region is as well known for its rich 6,000-year history as for its lyrical beauty. Kennet Country will be especially attractive to visitors in 1990 – a year in which the rescued and carefully restored Kennet and Avon Canal will reopen and celebrate its centenary. *Contact the Tourism Officer, Browfort, Bath Road, Devises, Wilts. Tel: Devises (0380) 729146.*

Ragley Hall

Mountfitchet Castle is an exciting and unique re-creation, on the original site, of a Norman motte-and-bailey castle and village. It's the castle that time forgot! *Mountfitchet Castle, Stansted, Essex. Tel: Bishop's Stortford (0279) 813237.*

The award-winning **Museum of Army Flying** tells the story of 100 years of army flight with vintage aircraft and imaginative display techniques. Licensed restaurant overlooking aircraft. *Museum of Army Flying, Middle Wallop, Stockbridge, Hampshire. Tel: Andover (0264) 62121 ext 4421.*

The National Caravan Council is the representative body of the British caravan industry. Its members are caravan manufacturers, dealers, park operators and suppliers. *Catherine House, Victoria Road, Aldershot, Hants. Tel: Aldershot (0252) 318251.*

National Express Ltd is Britain's largest coach company and runs scheduled services and special holiday services all over the country, as well as holidays in Great Britain and Europe. *Contact any local agent, or National Express in telephone directory. Head Office, Tel: Edgbaston (021 456) 1122.*

Ragley Hall, near Alcester, Warwickshire, is the ancestral home of the Marquis of Hertford and one of the loveliest of England's great Palladian country houses. It has a fine landscaped Victorian garden, a 400-acre park, a lake for fishing and watersports, a country trail and a popular adventure playground. *Tel: Alcester (0789) 762090.*

The Royal Air Force Museum at Grahame Park Way, Hendon, in London is Britain's only national museum of aviation. Here magnificent flying machines from Bleriot's day to the Lightning are displayed in the vast Aircraft Hall. *Tel: London (01 205) 2266.*

There are buildings at **Sudeley Castle** in Gloucestershire which date from the 12th-C., although the castle was rebuilt in 1441. See Charles I's giant four-poster bed and the christening gown worked by Anne Boleyn for the future Elizabeth I. *Sudley Castle, Winchcombe, Gloucestershire. Tel: Winchcombe (0242) 602308.*

Warwick Castle is a complete medieval castle, standing majestically beside the River Avon and surrounded by 'Capability' Brown parkland. See the staterooms, towers and dungeons and the private apartments of this living fortress. Here is one of the finest collections of armour in the country. *Tel: Warwick (0926) 495421.*

King Charles I's four-poster bed at Sudeley Castle

Guided Tours

Tourist guide services of various kinds are available in many parts of the region. The following organizations are members of the Tourist Board:

Berkshire

Thames and Chilterns Tourist Board Guides Association, Tel: Windsor (0753) 863667. A professional, local guiding service; several languages available.

Thames Valley V.I.P.s, Gates House, Garden Close Lane, Newbury. Tel: Newbury (0635) 32205.
Business hospitality and guided tours of the Thames Valley area for individuals and groups.

Walking Tours of Windsor leave the Information Centre, Central Station, mid-March to mid-November. Available to groups at any time of year. Tel: Windsor (0753) 852010.

Windsorian Coaches Ltd, 103 Arthur Road, Windsor. Tel: Windsor (0753) 856841. Royal Heritage Drive, a ten-mile, open-top bus tour departing from Castle Hill, Windsor, daily during the summer.

Buckinghamshire

Buckinghamshire Heritage Tours, 15 Bowlers Orchard, Chalfont St Giles. Tel: Chalfont St Giles (02407) 71080. A wide range of personally escorted regular, theme and custom-tailored tours in the Thames and Chilterns region.

Hertfordshire

City of St Albans Association of Honorary Guides, Tel: Tours Secretary, St Albans (0727) 33001; St Albans (0727) 64511. Guided walks and tours of Roman and medieval sights led by trained local guides.

Oxfordshire

Cotswold Experience, Thames Gardens, Charlbury, Oxon. Tel: Charlbury (0608) 810375. Personalised tours of the Cotswolds, including Stratford and Bath.

Guide Friday Ltd, Tourism Reception Centre, Oxford Railway Station. Tel: Oxford (0865) 790522. Frequent, daily tours of Oxford by double-decker bus.

Oxford Guild of Guide Lecturers. Tel: Abingdon (0235) 24109. Official guided tours of Oxford's sights by professional Blue Badge guides.

Oxford Language and Cultural Services, 82 The Paddocks, Yarnton. Tel: Kidlington (0865) 71722. Personalised courses emphasising cultural attractions and conversational English (2-week minimum).

Spires and Shires Minibus Tours, Tel: Oxford (0865) 513918, 727855. Eight-seat minibus tours of Oxford and surrounding countryside. Evening pub tours and excursions to Stratford.

T.C.C.L. Ltd, 27 Ditchley Road, Charlbury. Tel: Charlbury (0608) 810578. Personalised car tours and luxury minibus tours.

Official Walking Tours of Oxford leave Oxford Information Centre several times a day during the summer season and daily the rest of the year. Tel: Oxford (0865) 726871.

White's of Oxford Ltd, 53 Stanway Road, Risinghurst, Oxford. Tel: Oxford (0865) 61295. Private chauffeur-driven car and minibus tours, including Cotswold village tours.

Beyond the Region

Itinerant Tours Consultancy, Faulkners Road, Walton-on-Thames, Surrey. Tel: Weybridge (0932) 245988. Nostalgic tours in newly refurbished vintage buses.

Take A Guide Ltd, 11 Uxbridge Street, London, offers special trips for up to four persons in private cars or six in limousines. Tel: (01 221) 5475.

Mayflower Barn, Jordans

Tourist Information

Call in at one of our 39 friendly Tourist Information Centres for helpful information about accommodation, attractions and events. Whether it's the name of that special restaurant you can't remember, a hotel with a relaxing sauna you seek or suggestions on ways to enjoy a rainy day with the children, the trained TIC staff will make every effort to assist you.

Located in towns and cities all over the five-county Thames and Chilterns region, the information centres offer a comprehensive range of travel-related services, including a wide selection of regional and national literature, assistance with local accommodation and the popular Book a Bed Ahead scheme.

Abingdon
Ground Floor, Old Gaol Leisure Centre,
Bridge Street, OX14 3LS
Tel: Abingdon (0235) 22711

Ampthill
12 Dunstable Street, MK45 2JU
Tel: Ampthill (0525) 402051

Aylesbury
County Hall, Walton Street, HP20 1UA
Tel: (0296) 382308

Banbury
Banbury Museum, 8 Horsefair, OX6 0AA
Tel: Banbury (0295) 59855

Bedford
10 St Paul's Square, MK40 1SL
Tel: Bedford (0234) 215226

Berkhamsted
County Library, Kings Road, HP4 3BD
Tel: Berkhamsted (0442) 864545

Bishop's Stortford
Council Offices, 2 The Causeway, CM23 2EJ
Tel: Bishop's Stortford (0279) 655261 ext. 251

Borehamwood
Civic Offices, Elstree Way, WD6 1WA
Tel: (01 207) 2277 ext. 329

Bracknell
Central Library, Town Square, RG12 1BH
Tel: Bracknell (0344) 423149

Burford
Sheep Street, OX8 4LP
Tel: Burford (099382) 3558

Chipping Norton
New Street Car Park,
Tel: Chipping Norton (0608) 44379

Cropredy
Country Crafts, The Green.
Tel: Cropredy (0295) 758203

Dunstable
County Library, Vernon Place LU5 4HA
Tel: Dunstable (0582) 471012

Faringdon
The Pump House, 5 Market Place, SN7 7HL
Tel: Faringdon (0367) 22191
Open Easter–Oct only.

Hemel Hempstead
The Pavilion Box Office, Marlowes, HP1 1HA
Tel: Hemel Hempstead (0442) 64451

Henley
Town Hall, Market Place, RG9 2AQ
Tel: Henley (0491) 578034

Hertford
The Castle, SG14 1HR
Tel: Hertford (0992) 584322

High Wycombe
6 Cornmarket, HP11 2BW
Tel: High Wycombe (0494) 28652

Hitchin
County Library, Paynes Park, SG5 1EW
Tel: Hitchin (0462) 34738

Luton
Grosvenor House, 45/47A Alma Street, LU1 2PL
Tel: Luton (0582) 401579

Luton International Airport
Main Terminal, LU2 9LY
Tel: Luton (0582) 405100

Maidenhead
Central Library, Town Hall, St Ives Road, SL6 1QY
Tel: Maidenhead (0628) 781110

Marlow
Court Garden Leisure Complex, Higginson Park, Pound Lane
Tel: Marlow (06284) 3597.
Open Easter–Sept only.

Milton Keynes
Saxon Court, 502 Avebury Boulevard,
Central Milton Keynes, MK9 3HS
Tel: Milton Keynes (0908) 691995

Newbury
District Museum, The Wharf,
RG14 5AS
Tel: Newbury (0635) 30267

Oxford
St Aldate's, OX1 1DY
Tel: Oxford (0865) 726871

Reading
Museum Art Gallery,
Blagrave Street, RG1 1QH
Tel: Reading (0734) 399811

Rickmansworth
46 High Street, WD1 1HJ
Tel: Rickmansworth (0923) 776611

St Albans
Town Hall, The Market Place, AL3
5DJ
Tel: St Albans (0727) 64511

South Mimms
M25 Service Area, Bignells Corner,
MK9 3HS
Tel: Potters Bar (0707) 43233

Stevenage
Central Library, Southgate, SG1
1HD
Tel: Stevenage (0438) 369441

Thame
Town Hall, OX9 3DP
Tel: Thame (084421) 2834

Wallingford
9 St Martin's Street, OX10 OAL
Tel: Wallingford (0491) 35351 ext
3810

Welwyn Garden City
Campus West, The Campus, AL8
6BX
Tel: Welwyn Garden (0707) 332880

Wendover
The Clock Tower, HP22 6DU
Tel: Wendover (0296) 623056

Windsor
Central Station, Thames Street,
SL4 1QU
Tel: Windsor (0753) 852010

Witney
Town Hall, Market Square, OX8
6AG
Tel: Witney (0993) 775802

Heritage Centre, Woburn
9 Bedford Street, MK17 9QB
Personal callers only.

Woodstock
Hensington Road, OX7 1JQ
Tel: Woodstock (0993) 811038

Publications

The Thames and Chilterns Tourist Board produces a variety of publications, some of which may be ordered by completing the form below and returning it to:

Marketing Department, Thames and Chilterns Tourist Board, The Mount House, Church Green, Witney, Oxon OX8 6DZ

------✂--

Please send me the following publications (prices include p&p)

Leisure Map
Official Tourist Map of the Region
£2.95 ☐

Welcome to Oxford
The definitive map, walking tour and guide
75p ☐

Churches of the Thames and Chilterns
Nearly 100 lesser-known gems
50p ☐

Historic Houses in the Thames and Chilterns
An informative leaflet with 1990 details
Free ☐

A Cottage in the Country
The Region's self-catering holiday brochure
Free ☐

Name _____

Address _____

_____ Postcode _____

Guide to Accommodation

All members of Thames and Chilterns Tourist Board are also registered with the English Tourist Board. The prices quoted are per room per night (two people sharing a double/twin) and were correct at the time of publication; however, details should be checked when booking.

CROWN CLASSIFICATION SCHEME – Hotels, Guesthouses, Motels, Inns, B&Bs, Farmhouses

Over 16,000 hotels, guesthouses, motels, inns, B&Bs and farmhouses throughout England, Scotland and Wales now offer the reassurance of a national Crown classification – and the number grows daily.

Whatever the classification, ranging from 'Listed' to Five Crown, every classified establishment is inspected by the tourist boards each year to make sure that standards have been maintained.

More Crowns simply mean a wider range of facilities and services. A lower classification does not imply lower standards. Although the range of facilities and services may be smaller, they may be provided to a high standard.

Classifications are subject to change. Those that appear in this guide were correct at the time the entries were accepted.

●	Clean and comfortable accommodation, although the range of facilities and services may be limited
♛	Accommodation with additional facilities, including washbasins in all bedrooms, a lounge area and use of a telephone
♛ ♛	A wider range of facilities and services, including morning tea/coffee and calls, bedside lights, colour TV in lounge or bedrooms, assistance with luggage
♛ ♛ ♛	At least one-third of the bedrooms with ensuite WC and bath or shower, plus easy chair and full length mirror, shoe cleaning facilities and hairdryers available
♛ ♛ ♛ ♛	At least three-quarters of the bedrooms with ensuite WC and bath or shower plus colour TV, radio and telephone, 24-hour access and lounge service until midnight
♛ ♛ ♛ ♛ ♛	All bedrooms having WC, bath and shower ensuite, trouser press (or valet service) plus a wide range of facilities and services, including room service, all-night lounge service and laundry service

Looking Ahead

To help you find accommodation that offers even higher standards than those required for a simple classification, the English Tourist Board is introducing three levels of quality commendation using the terms Approved, Commended and Highly Commended. When granted these will appear alongside the classification.

The new quality commendations will apply to all the classification bands. A 'Listed' or One Crown B&B or guest house may be Commended or even Highly Commended if its facilities and services, although limited in range, are provided to a high quality standard.

This new arrangement is being introduced progressively during 1990. In the meantime you will begin to see the terms Approved, Commended and Highly Commended on English Tourist Board classification signs.

Serviced Accommodation – Key to Symbols

⋈	No. of single rooms		℗	Parking	
♨	No. of double/twin rooms		SB	Short breaks	
F	No. of family rooms		⚘	Christmas/New Year breaks	
⊞	No. of en-suite bathrooms		🏛	Building of historic interest	
♿	Disabled access		⊟	Four-poster beds	
⅗	Children welcome (min. age if any)		☺	Leisure/sports facilities	
♀	Liquor licence		⚒	Conference facilities	
⊞	Credit cards accepted				

HOLIDAY HOMES APPROVAL SCHEME
– Self-catering holiday homes Ⓐ

Over 10,000 holiday homes in England have been inspected and "Approved" by the tourist boards. All have been found to meet satisfactory standards of cleanliness and maintenance and to provide an adequate range of facilities and equipment.

"Approved" status is subject to being withdrawn if standards are not maintained. All "Approved" entries in this guide were correct at the time the entry was accepted.

Looking Ahead to 'Key' changes

During 1990 the English Tourist Board will be developing the scheme to make it even more helpful when choosing a self-catering holiday home. Under the new arrangement, the range of facilities and equipment provided will be indicated by 'Key' symbols, from One Key to Five Keys – the more Keys, the more extensive the range of facilities and equipment.

Those places offering higher quality standards than those required for a simple 'Key' classification will be distinguished by the terms Approved, Commended and Highly Commended appearing alongside the 'Key' symbols. A One Key holiday home can be Highly Commended if its facilities and equipment – although limited in range – are provided to a very high quality standard.

The new arrangement is being introduced progressively. In the meantime you will begin to see the new 'Key' symbols and the terms Approved, Commended and Highly Commended appear on English Tourist Board signs.

Self-Catering – Key to Symbols

♿	Disabled facilities	M	Metered fuel	
⅗	Children welcome (min. age if any)	◙	Washing machine available	
℗	Parking	⊡	Colour television	
◎	Cooking by electricity	⊞	Linen available	
∂	Cooking by gas	🐕	Dog accepted by arrangement	
▥	Central heating throughout	4–10	Months open, e.g. Apr–Oct	

BRITISH GRADED HOLIDAY PARKS SCHEME
– Holiday caravan, chalet and camping parks

Over 1,000 holiday parks throughout England, Scotland and Wales now offer the reassurance of a national quality grade. All are inspected annually by the tourist boards. All graded parks can be chosen with confidence.

There are five grades, indicated by 1–5 ticks. The more ticks the higher the quality standard. Even a small, quiet park with few facilities can achieve 5 ticks if what it offers is to an exceptionally high quality standard.

Camping and Caravanning – Key to Symbols

⊞	Motor caravans accepted	⅊	Foodshop in site	
▣	Flush toilets on site	ℓ	Public telephone on site	
♀	Liquor licence	◙	Washing machine available	
⚘	Showers available	🐕	Dog accepted by arrangement	
⚙	Electric hook-up supply for caravans	4–10	Months open, e.g. Apr–Oct	

HOTELS, GUEST HOUSES, FARMHOUSES, INNS, B&B

Establishment Name & Address	Crown Classification	Bedroom Numbers and Facilities	Prices (£) MIN MAX	

Bedfordshire

Establishment Name & Address	Crown Classification	Bedroom Numbers and Facilities	MIN	MAX
Moore Place, The Square, **Aspley Guise**, Nr. Woburn, MK17 8DW ☎ (0908) 282000	♛♛♛♛♛	18⊨ 35♯ 1F 54⊞ ♿ ⛵ ⛵ ⊞ ⋈ SB ⛩ ✪ ⛾	75.00 85.00	80.00 95.00
Barns Hotel, Cardington Road, **Bedford**, MK44 3SA ☎ (0234) 270044		47♯ 2F 49⊞ ♿ ⛵ ⛵ ⊞ ⋈ SB ⚲ ⛩ ⛾	55.00 65.00	— —
Bedford Moat House, St. Mary's Street, **Bedford**, MK42 0AR ☎ (0234) 55131		31⊨ 48♯ 21F 100⊞ ♿ ⛵ ⛵ ⊞ ⋈ SB ⛾	57.50 75.00	— —
Bedford Swan Hotel, The Embankment, **Bedford**, MK40 1RW ☎ (0234) 46565	♛♛♛♛♛	31⊨ 53♯ 2F 86⊞ ⛵ ⛵ ⊞ ⋈ SB ⚲ ⛩ ✪ ⛾	— —	59.00 69.00
Kimbolton Hotel, 78 Clapham Road, **Bedford**, MK41 7PN ☎ (0234) 54854	♛♛♛	9⊨ 5♯ 14⊞ ⛵3 ⛵ ⊞ ⋈ SB ⛾	23.00 34.50	33.75 43.70
The Knife and Cleaver, Houghton Conquest, **Bedford**, MK45 3LA ☎ (0234) 740387	♛♛	6♯ 6⊞ ⛵ ⛵ ⊞ ⋈ ⛩ ⛾	32.00 40.00	32.00 40.00
The Queens Head Hotel, 2 Rushden Road, Milton Ernest, **Bedford**, MK44 1RV ☎ (0234) 272822	♛♛♛♛	2⊨ 11♯ 14⊞ ♿ ⛵ ⛵ ⊞ ⋈ SB ⛩ ⛾	49.00 66.00	52.50 68.00
Woodlands Manor, Green Lane, Clapham, **Bedford**, MK41 6EP ☎ (0234) 63281		4⊨ 25♯ 29⊞ ⛵7 ⛵ ⊞ ⋈ SB ⚲ ⛩ ⛾	42.00 56.00	59.75 89.50
Stratton House Hotel, London Road, **Biggleswade**, SG18 8EO ☎ (0767) 312442 & 314540	♛♛♛	14⊨ 16♯ 5F 29⊞ ⛵ ⛵ ⊞ ⋈ SB ⛩ ⛾	28.00 45.00	40.00 50.00
Cranfield Conference Centre, Wharley End, **Cranfield**, MK43 0HG ☎ (0234) 751077		106⊨ 6♯ 112⊞ ♿ ⛵ ⛵ ⊞ ⋈ ✪ ⛾	48.00 58.00	— —
Highwayman Hotel, London Road, **Dunstable**, LU6 3DX ☎ (0582) 661999	♛♛♛♛	24⊨ 14♯ 38⊞ ⛵ ⛵ ⊞ ⋈ SB ⛾	43.00 53.00	— —
Old Palace Lodge Hotel, Church Street, **Dunstable**, LU5 5LL ☎ (0582) 662201	♛♛♛♛♛	5⊨ 44♯ 0F 49⊞ ⛵ ⛵ ⊞ ⋈ SB ⚲ ⛩ ⛾ ⛾	59.50 65.00	— —
Priory Guest House, 30 Priory Road, **Dunstable**, LU5 4HR ☎ (0582) 661900	♛♛	2⊨ 5♯ 1F ⛵ ⊞	16.00 28.00	— —

Establishment Name & Address	Crown Classification	Bedroom Numbers and Facilities	Prices (£) MIN	MAX
Leaways, Grange Road, **Felmersham**, MK43 7EU ☎ (0234) 781430	♛♛	2♛ 2⊞ 🅿	20.00 35.00	20.00 35.00
Flitwick Manor, Church Road, **Flitwick**, MK45 1AE ☎ (0525) 712242	♛♛♛♛	3♙ 12♛ 15⊞ ⌂ ♀ ⊞ 🅿 SB ⌖ ⊟ ✪ 𝍖	70.00 90.00	125.00 160.00
The Cock Horse Hotel, Woburn Road, **Heath and Reach**, Leighton Buzzard ☎ (052523) 7816/7817/7818		16♛ 16⊞ ♿ ⌂ ♀ ⊞ SB	23.00 29.50	40.00 50.00
Swan Hotel, High Street, **Leighton Buzzard**, LU7 7EA ☎ (0525) 372148	♛♛♛♛	22♙ 15♛ 1𝔽 38⊞ ⌂ ♀ ⊞ 🅿 SB ⌖ 𝍖	59.50 72.00	65.00 80.00
Adelphia Hotel, 18 Conway Road, **Luton**, LU4 8JA ☎ (0582) 23689		6♙ 60♛ 4𝔽 3⊞ ⌂ ♀ ⊞ 🅿	18.00 30.00	20.00 36.00
Chiltern Crest Hotel, Waller Avenue, Dunstable Road, **Luton**, LU4 9RU ☎ (0582) 575911		3♙ 93♛ 96⊞ ♿ ⌂ ♀ ⊞ 🅿 SB 𝍖	85.00 106.00	— —
Crest Hotel, Dunstable Road, **Luton**, LU4 8RQ ☎ (0582) 575955		71♙ 46♛ 117♙ ♿ ⌂ ♀ ⊞ 🅿 SB 𝍖	81.00 101.00	— —
Pines Hotel, 10 Marsh Road, Leagrave, **Luton**, LU3 2NH ☎ (0582) 575552	♛	8♙ 10♛ 2𝔽 ⌂ ♀ ⊞ 🅿 SB ⊟	18.00 30.00	20.00 36.00
Red Lion Hotel, Castle Street, **Luton**, LU1 3AA ☎ (0582) 413881	♛♛♛♛	9♙ 27♛ 2𝔽 38⊞ ♿ ⌂ ♀ ⊞ 🅿 SB ⊟ 𝍖	57.00 67.00	— —
Strathmore Thistle Hotel, Arndale Centre, **Luton**, LU1 2TR ☎ (0582) 34199	♛♛♛	33♙ 114♛ 3𝔽 150⊞ ♿ ⌂ ♀ ⊞ 🅿 SB 𝍖	70.25 89.50	87.25 107.50
Malletts, Great Farm, Silsoe Road, **Maulden**, MK45 2AZ ☎ (0525) 402248		6♛ 6⊞ ♀ ⊞ 🅿 SB ⌖ ✪ 𝍖	69.00 115.00	— 190.00
Fairlawn Hotel, 70 Bedford Road, **Sandy**, SG19 1EP ☎ (0767) 80336		4♙ 3♛ 1𝔽 1⊞ ⌂ ♀ ⊞ 🅿 SB	22.50 35.00	27.50 38.00
Rose & Crown Hotel, Market Square, Potton, **Sandy**, SG19 2NP ☎ (0767) 260221 & 260409	♛♛	4♙ 8♛ 3𝔽 10⊞ ⌂ ♀ ⊞ 🅿 SB ⌖ 𝍖	20.00 32.00	30.00 40.00
Sandy Motel, Girtford Bridge, London Road, **Sandy**, SG19 1DH ☎ (0767) 292220	♛♛	12♛ 37𝔽 49⊞ ♿ ⌂ ⊞ 🅿 SB 𝍖	29.00 33.00	41.50 47.50

Establishment Name & Address	Crown Classification	Bedroom Numbers and Facilities	Prices (£) MIN MAX
Beadlow Manor Hotel, Golf and Country Club, 2 Ampthill Road, Beadlow, Nr. **Shefford**, SG17 5PH ☎ (0525) 60800	♕ ♕	20♔ 20⊞ ⟶ ♀ ⊞ 🅿 SB ⚲ ♟	⇌ 29.00 55.00 ⚏ 39.00 68.00
The Anchor Hotel, Great North Road, **Tempsford**, Sandy, SG19 2AS ☎ (0767) 40233		2⇥ 8♔ 8⊞ ⟶ ♀ ⊞ 🅿 SB ⚱ ♟	⇌ 33.00 41.00 ⚏ 52.50 52.50
Bedford Arms Hotel, George Street, **Woburn**, MK17 9PX ☎ (0525) 290441	♕ ♕ ♕ ♕ ♕	3⇥ 48♔ 4⧆ 55⊞ ♿ ⟶ ⊞ 🅿 SB ⚲ ⚱ ▤ ♟	⇌ 32.50 67.50 ⚏ — —
The Bell Inn, 21 Bedford Street, **Woburn**, MK17 9QD ☎ (0525) 290280	♕ ♕ ♕ ♕	13⇥ 10♔ 2⧆ 25⊞ ⟶ ♀ ⊞ 🅿 SB ⚲ ⚱ ♟	⇌ 30.00 45.00 ⚏ 42.50 58.00
Wyboston Lakes Motel, Great North Road, **Wyboston**, MK44 3AL ☎ (0480) 219949/214046	♕ ♕	38⇥ 38⊞ ⟶ ♀ ⊞ 🅿 SB ♟	⇌ 29.00 42.50 ⚏ 33.00 48.50

Berkshire

Establishment Name & Address	Crown Classification	Bedroom Numbers and Facilities	Prices (£) MIN MAX
The Berystede, Bagshot Road, Sunninghill, **Ascot**, SL5 9JH ☎ (0990) 23311		26⇥ 59♔ 6⧆ 91⊞ ⟶ ♀ ⊞ 🅿 SB ⚲ ⚱ ♟	⇌ 81.00 96.00 ⚏ 102.00 145.00
Brockenhurst Hotel, Brockenhurst Road, South **Ascot**, SL5 9HA ☎ (0990) 21912		1⇥ 8♔ 2⧆ ⟶ ⊞ 🅿	⇌ — 50.00 ⚏ — 60.00
Highclere Hotel, Kings Road, Sunninghill, **Ascot**, SL5 9AD ☎ (0990) 25220	♕ ♕ ♕	11♔ 8⊞ ⟶ ♀ ⊞ 🅿 SB ▤ ♟	⇌ 36.00 59.00 ⚏ 44.00 65.00
The Royal Berkshire Hotel, Sunninghill, **Ascot**, SL5 0PP ☎ (0990) 23322	♕ ♕ ♕ ♕ ♕	15⇥ 67♔ 65⊞ ⟶ ♀ ⊞ 🅿 SB ⚲ ▤ ✪ ♟	⇌ — — ⚏ — —
Hilton National Bracknell, Bagshot Road, **Bracknell**, RG12 3QJ ☎ (0344) 424801	♕ ♕ ♕ ♕ ♕	25⇥ 122♔ 147⊞ ♿ ⟶ ♀ ⊞ 🅿 SB ✪ ♟	⇌ 80.00 96.00 ⚏ 86.00 —
Manor Farm, **Brimpton**, Nr. Reading, RG7 4SQ ☎ (0734) 713166	🅛	2♔ ⟶ 🅿 ▤	⇌ 13.00 16.50 ⚏ 26.00 35.00
Dial House Private Hotel, 62 Dukes Ride, **Crowthorne**, RG11 6DL ☎ (0344) 776941	♕ ♕ ♕ ♕	6⇥ 7♔ 3⧆ 14⊞ ⟶ ♀ ⊞ 🅿 SB ♟	⇌ 24.00 53.00 ⚏ 42.00 58.00
Waterloo Hotel, Duke's Ride, **Crowthorne**, RG11 7NW ☎ (0344) 777711	26⇥ 32♔ 58⊞ ♿ ⟶ ♀ ⊞ 🅿 SB ▤ ♟		⇌ 70.00 75.00 ⚏ 80.00 85.00

Establishment Name & Address	Crown Classification	Bedroom Numbers and Facilities	Prices (£) MIN	MAX
The Manor Hotel, The Green, **Datchet**, SL3 9EA ☎ (0753) 43442	♔♔♔♔	7🛏 22♔ 1🄵 30⊞ 🛋 ♉ 🄴 🅿 SB ✎ 🎠 🚗 ⵏ	🛏 49.00 ⵏ 69.00	59.00 —
Yaffles, Red Shute Hill, **Hermitage**, Nr. Newbury, RG16 9QH ☎ (0635) 201100	♔♔	1🄵 1⊞ 🛋 🅿 SB	🛏 22.00 ⵏ 28.00	27.00 33.00
Bear Hotel & Restaurant, Charnham Street, **Hungerford**, RG17 0EL ☎ (0488) 82512	♔♔♔♔	3🛏 35♔ 3🄵 41⊞ ♿ 🛋 ♉ 🄴 🅿 SB ✎ 🎠 🚗 ⊕ ⵏ	🛏 55.95 ⵏ 71.90	65.95 81.90
Marshgate Cottage, Marsh Lane, **Hungerford**, RG17 0QX ☎ (0488) 82307	♔♔	1🛏 6♔ 2🄵 7⊞ 🛋5 🅿 🚗 ⊕ ⵏ	🛏 22.50 ⵏ 31.50	31.50 43.50
Ye Olde Bell, **Hurley**, Nr. Maidenhead, SL6 5LX ☎ (062882) 5881/4		7🛏 15♔ 3🄵 25⊞ 🛋 ♉ 🄴 🅿 SB ✎ 🎠 🚗 ⵏ	🛏 62.00 ⵏ 83.00	— —
Bird In Hand, Bath Road, **Knowl Hill**, Twyford, Nr. Reading, RG10 9UP ☎ (062882) 2781/6622	♔♔♔♔	1🛏 14♔ 15⊞ ♿ 🛋 ♉ 🄴 🅿 SB ⵏ	🛏 40.00 ⵏ 50.00	65.00 80.00
Boulters' Lock Inn, Boulters' Lock, **Maidenhead**, SL6 8PE ☎ (0628) 21291	🅛	2🛏 12♔ 1🄵 12⊞ 🛋 ♉ 🄴 🅿 SB 🎠 🚗 ⵏ	🛏 65.00 ⵏ 85.00	125.00 175.00
Copperfields Guest House, 54 Bath Road, **Maidenhead**, SL6 4JY ☎ (0628) 74941		3🛏 2♔ 2⊞ 🛋10 🄴 🅿	🛏 21.00 ⵏ 31.00	25.00 35.00
Crest Hotel, Manor Lane, **Maidenhead**, SL6 2RA ☎ (0628) 23444		183♔ 6🄵 189⊞ ♿ 🛋 ♉ 🄴 🅿 SB ✎ 🎠 🚗 ⊕ ⵏ	🛏 93.00 ⵏ 113.00	— —
Frederick's Hotel & Restaurant, Shoppenhangers Road, **Maidenhead**, SL6 2PZ ☎ (0628) 35934 & 24737		10🛏 27♔ 1🄵 38⊞ 🛋 ♉ 🄴 🅿 ⵏ	🛏 83.00 ⵏ 121.00	95.00 204.00
Kingswood Hotel, Boyn Hill Avenue, **Maidenhead**, SL6 4EN ☎ (0628) 33598	♔♔♔♔	4🛏 11♔ 2🄵 17⊞ ♿ 🛋 ♉ 🄴 🅿 SB ✎ 🎠 🚗 ⵏ	🛏 40.00 ⵏ 65.00	65.00 85.00
Monkey Island Hotel, Bray-on-Thames, **Maidenhead**, SL6 2EE ☎ (0628) 23400		2🛏 23♔ 2🄵 27⊞ ♿ 🛋 ♉ 🄴 🅿 SB ✎ 🎠 ⵏ	🛏 72.00 ⵏ 94.00	83.00 105.00
Norfolk House Hotel and Restaurant, 4 Bath Road, Taplow, **Maidenhead**, SL6 0AP ☎ (0628) 23687/784031	♔♔♔♔	2🛏 8♔ 10⊞ 🛋 ♉ 🄴 🅿 SB 🎠 ⊕ ⵏ	🛏 45.00 ⵏ 80.00	55.00 85.00
Ray Corner Guest House, 141 Bridge Road, **Maidenhead**, SL6 8NQ ☎ (0628) 32784	🅛	1🛏 2♔ 1🄵 1⊞ 🛋1 🅿	🛏 15.00 ⵏ 30.00	18.00 34.00

Establishment Name & Address	Crown Classification	Bedroom Numbers and Facilities	Prices (£) MIN	MAX
Taplow House Hotel, Berry Hill, Taplow, **Maidenhead**, SL6 0DA ☎ (0628) 70056	♛♛♛♛	11 13 4 28 / SB	65.00 90.00	75.00 105.00
Thames Hotel, Ray Mead Road, **Maidenhead**, SL6 8NR ☎ (0628) 28721		21 12 33 / SB	30.00 60.00	54.00 75.00
The Thames Riviera Hotel, At The Bridge, **Maidenhead**, SL6 8DW ☎ (0628) 74057	♛♛♛	7 40 3 50 / SB	— —	80.00 95.00
The Blue Boar Inn, North Heath, Nr. Chieveley, **Newbury**, RG16 8UE ☎ (0635) 248236/248176		6 12 16 / SB	55.00 60.00	60.00 70.00
The Chequers, Oxford Street, **Newbury**, RG13 1JB ☎ (0635) 38000		1 36 3 56 / SB	62.00 85.00	80.00 105.00
Elcot Park Resort Hotel, Kintbury, Nr. **Newbury**, RG16 8NJ ☎ (0488) 58100	♛♛♛♛	3 33 1 37 / SB	63.00 70.00	85.00 68.00
Enborne Grange Hotel, Enborne Street, Wash Common, **Newbury**, RG14 6RP ☎ (0635) 40046 & 41237	♛♛♛♛	5 20 1 26 / SB	38.00 58.00	60.00 68.00
Foley Lodge Hotel, Stockcross, **Newbury**, RG16 8JU ☎ (0635) 528770		70 70 7 / SB	84.50 109.60	84.50 109.60
Hilton National Hotel, Pinchington Lane, **Newbury**, RG14 7HL ☎ (0635) 529000		107 17 114 / SB	35.00 70.00	90.00 120.00
Millwaters Hotel, London Road, **Newbury**, RG13 2BY ☎ (0635) 49977	♛♛♛♛	17 17 12 / SB	64.00 79.00	— —
Stakis Newbury Hotel, Oxford Road, **Newbury**, RG16 8XY ☎ (0635) 247010		110 2 112 / SB	36.00 52.00	75.00 99.00
The Copper Inn, Church Road, **Pangbourne**, RG8 7AR ☎ (07357) 2244	♛♛♛♛	2 18 1 21 / SB	60.95 76.90	65.95 81.90
The George Hotel, The Square, **Pangbourne**, Nr. Reading, RG8 7AJ ☎ (07357) 2237 & 4354	♛♛	9 8 8 / SB	34.25 58.50	54.25 63.50
Abbey House Private Hotel, 118 Connaught Road, **Reading**, RG3 2UF ☎ (0734) 590549	♛♛	10 9 4	21.50 36.00	35.00 44.00

Establishment Name & Address	Crown Classification	Bedroom Numbers and Facilities	Prices (£) MIN MAX	
Aeron Private Hotel, 191 Kentwood Hill, Tilehurst, **Reading**, RG3 6JE ☎ (0734) 424119 & 427654	♛ ♛	13🛏 5🛁 1🅵 ⌕ ♀ 🅴 🅿	24.00 37.00	38.00 48.00
Calcot Hotel, 98 Bath Road, Calcot, **Reading**, RG3 5QN ☎ (0734) 416423		28🛏 13🛁 1🅵 25⊡ ⌕ ♀ 🅴 🅿 SB 🎏 ⚷	51.50 68.00	58.50 75.00
Caversham Hotel, Caversham Bridge, Richfield Avenue, Caversham, **Reading**, RG1 8BD ☎ (0734) 391818	♛ ♛ ♛ ♛ ♛	1🛏 99🛁 8🅵 108⊡ ♿ ⌕ ♀ 🅴 🅿 SB ✂ ◑ ⚷	87.00 87.00	87.00 87.00
George Hotel, King Street, **Reading**, RG1 2HE ☎ (0734) 573445	♛ ♛ ♛	19🛏 47🛁 2🅵 68⊡ ⌕ ♀ 🅴 SB 🎠 🎏 ⚷	49.00 61.00	49.00 61.00
Kirtons Farm Country Club & Hotel, Pingewood, **Reading**, RG3 3UN ☎ (0734) 500885	♛ ♛ ♛ ♛ ♛	30🛁 30⊡ ♿ ⌕ ♀ 🅴 🅿 SB ✂ 🎠 ◑ ⚷	64.00 79.00	— —
Post House Hotel, Basingstoke Road, **Reading**, RG2 0SL ☎ (0734) 875485		29🛏 71🛁 43🅵 143⊡ ♿ ⌕ ♀ 🅴 🅿 SB ✂ 🎏 ◑ ⚷	38.00 48.00	92.00 102.50
Rainbow Corner Hotel, 132–138 Caversham Road, **Reading**, RG1 8AY ☎ (0734) 588140 & 581542	♛ ♛ ♛ ♛	4🛏 15🛁 1🅵 20⊡ ⌕ ♀ 🅴 🅿 SB ✂ 🎠 🎏 ⚷	51.00 57.00	52.00 58.00
Ramada Hotel, Oxford Road, **Reading**, RG1 7RH ☎ (0734) 586222	♛ ♛ ♛ ♛ ♛	62🛏 138🛁 200⊡ ♿ ⌕ ♀ 🅴 SB ◑ ⚷	45.00 60.00	85.00 101.50
Ship Hotel, 4–8 Duke Street, **Reading**, RG1 4RU ☎ (0734) 583455		20🛏 12🛁 22⊡ ⌕ ♀ 🅴 ⚷	55.00 63.00	55.00 63.00
Upcross Hotel, 68 Berkeley Avenue, **Reading**, RG1 6HY ☎ (0734) 590796 & 391573	♛ ♛ ♛ ♛	13🛏 13🛁 1🅵 20⊡ ⌕ ♀ 🅴 🅿 SB 🎠 🎏 ⚷	45.00 65.00	55.00 65.00
The Willows Hotel, Bath Road, Padworth, Nr. **Reading**, RG7 5HT ☎ (0734) 713282	♛ ♛	6🛏 18🛁 24⊡ ⌕ ♀ 🅴 🅿 SB ✂ ⚷	40.00 55.00	— —
Heathrow Ambassador, London Road, Colnbrook, **Slough**, SL3 8QB ☎ (0753) 684001	♛ ♛ ♛	92🛏 10🅵 112⊡ ⌕ ♀ 🅴 🅿 SB ⚷	— —	57.50 90.00
Highways Guest House, 95 London Road, Langley, **Slough**, SL3 7RS ☎ (0753) 24715 & 23022	♛	2🛏 6🛁 2🅵 ⌕ 🅿 SB 🎠	20.00 30.00	— —
Holiday Inn – Slough/Windsor, Ditton Road, Langley, **Slough**, SL3 8PT ☎ (0753) 44244	♛ ♛ ♛ ♛ ♛	170🛁 132🅵 302⊡ ♿ ⌕ ♀ 🅴 🅿 SB ✂ ◑ ⚷	55.00 70.00	90.00 110.00

93

Establishment Name & Address	Crown Classification	Bedroom Numbers and Facilities	Prices (£) MIN MAX
Sussex Lodge Guest House, 91 Sussex Place, **Slough**, SL1 1NN ☎ (0753) 825674/825673		7🛏 7🛁 1🅵 2🔲 ⌂ ⚲ 📺 🅿 SB 🍴	⋈ 23.00 28.75 ⋈ 33.35 46.00
Butchers Arms, Blounts Court Road, **Sonning Common**, Nr Reading, RG4 9RS ☎ (0734) 723101	♔ ♔	1🛏 2🛁 ⌂5 ⚲ 📺 🅿 🍴	⋈ 15.00 25.00 ⋈ 30.00 50.00
The Great House at Sonning, Thames Street, **Sonning on Thames**, Nr. Reading, RG4 0UT ☎ (0734) 692277	♔ ♔ ♔ ♔	2🛏 52🛁 1🅵 55🔲 ⌂ ⚲ 📺 🅿 SB 🐾 🎮 📠 🍴	⋈ 69.00 79.00 ⋈ 79.00 99.00
The Swan Diplomat, **Streatley**, RG8 9HR ☎ (0491) 873737		12🛏 31🛁 43🔲 ♿ ⌂ ⚲ 📺 🅿 SB 🐾 🎮 ☻ 🍴	⋈ 75.00 97.00 ⋈ 105.00 198.00
The Mill House, Old Basingstoke Road, **Swallowfield**, Nr Reading, RG7 1PY ☎ (0734) 883124	♔ ♔ ♔ ♔	5🛏 4🛁 1🅵 10🔲 ⌂ ⚲ 📺 🅿 SB 🎮 📠 ☻ 🍴	⋈ 65.75 — ⋈ 83.50 93.50
Regency Park Hotel, Bowling Green Road, **Thatcham**, Nr. Newbury, RG13 3RP ☎ (0635) 71555	♔ ♔ ♔ ♔ ♔	20🛏 30🛁 50🔲 ♿ ⌂ ⚲ 📺 🅿 SB 🐾 🍴	⋈ 72.00 85.95 ⋈ 91.00 103.90
The Warrener Restaurant, Warren Row, Nr. **Wargrave**, RG10 8QS ☎ (062882) 6750	♔ ♔ ♔ ♔	5🛁 5🔲 ⌂7 ⚲ 📺 🅿 SB 🍴	⋈ — 75.00 ⋈ — 85.00
Aurora Garden Hotel, Bolton Avenue, **Windsor**, SL4 3JF ☎ (0753) 868686	♔ ♔ ♔ ♔	3🛏 10🛁 1🅵 14🔲 ⌂ ⚲ 📺 🅿 SB 🐾 🍴	⋈ 59.50 64.50 ⋈ 70.00 70.00
Castle Hotel, High Street, **Windsor**, SL4 1LJ ☎ (0753) 851011		19🛏 66🛁 85🔲 ⌂ ⚲ 📺 🅿 SB 🐾 📠 🍴	⋈ 56.00 78.00 ⋈ — —
The Christopher Hotel, 110 High Street, Eton, **Windsor**, SL4 6AN ☎ (0753) 852359		2🛏 27🛁 6🅵 35🔲 ⌂ ⚲ 📺 🅿 SB	⋈ 71.75 — ⋈ 95.00 —
Oakley Court Hotel, Windsor Road, Water Oakley, **Nr. Windsor**, SL4 5UR ☎ (0628) 74141	♔ ♔ ♔ ♔ ♔	92🛁 92🔲 ⌂ ⚲ 📺 🅿 SB 🎮 📠 🍴	⋈ 99.00 — ⋈ 119.00 —
Royal Adelaide Hotel, Kings Road, **Windsor**, SL4 2AG ☎ (0753) 863916	♔ ♔ ♔ ♔	20🛏 21🛁 1🅵 42🔲 ⌂ ⚲ 📺 🅿 SB 🐾 🎮 🍴	⋈ 55.00 67.00 ⋈ 65.00 80.00
Runnymede Hotel, Windsor Road, Egham, **Windsor**, TW20 0AG ☎ (0784) 436171	♔ ♔ ♔ ♔ ♔	48🛏 45🛁 32🅵 125🔲 ♿ ⌂ ⚲ 📺 🅿 SB 🐾 ☻ 🍴	⋈ 75.00 87.00 ⋈ 87.00 97.00
Sir Christopher Wren's House Hotel, 4 Thames Street, **Windsor**, SL4 1PX ☎ (0753) 861354	♔ ♔ ♔ ♔	6🛏 31🛁 37🔲 ⌂ ⚲ 📺 🅿 SB 🐾 🎮 📠 🍴	⋈ 79.00 99.00 ⋈ 99.00 120.00

Establishment Name & Address	Crown Classification	Bedroom Numbers and Facilities	Prices (£) MIN MAX	
Ye Harte and Garter Hotel, High Street, **Windsor**, SL4 1PH ☎ (0753) 863426	♛ ♛ ♛ ♛	16🛏 26🛁 8🅵 43🚿 ♿ 🏊 ♀ 🖸 SB 🗲 🍴 ⚓	🛏 39.50 47.00 🛁 69.50 69.50	
Cantley House, Milton Road, **Wokingham**, RG11 5QG ☎ (0734) 789912	♛ ♛ ♛ ♛	14🛏 13🛁 2🅵 29🚿 🗑 ♀ 🖸 🅿 SB 🍴 🚭 ⊕ ⚓	🛏 40.00 56.00 🛁 50.00 62.00	
Edward Court Hotel, Wellington Road, **Wokingham**, RG11 2AN ☎ (0734) 775886	♛ ♛	8🛏 17🛁 25🚿 ♿ ♀ 🖸 🅿 SB ⚓	🛏 52.00 58.00 🛁 65.00 68.00	
Reading Moat House, Mill Lane, Sindlesham, **Wokingham**, RG11 5DF ☎ (0734) 351035	♛ ♛ ♛ ♛ ♛	86🛁 10🅵 96🚿 🗑 ♀ 🖸 🅿 SB ⚓	🛏 89.50 91.50 🛁 99.00 103.00	
Stakis St. Anne's Manor Hotel, London Road, **Wokingham**, RG11 1ST ☎ (0734) 772550		9🛏 124🛁 133🚿 ♿ 🗑 ♀ 🖸 🅿 SB 🍴 🚭 ⊕ ⚓	🛏 86.00 — 🛁 110.00 —	
Chiltern Chase Lodge Hotel, Goring Road, **Woodcote**, Nr. Reading, RG8 0SD ☎ (0491) 680775		3🛏 2🛁 🗑 ♀ 🅿 ⚓	🛏 19.50 — 🛁 36.20 —	

Buckinghamshire

Establishment Name & Address	Crown Classification	Bedroom Numbers and Facilities	Prices (£) MIN MAX	
The Crown, High Street, **Amersham**, HP7 0DH ☎ (0494) 721541		4🛏 21🛁 14🚿 🗑 ♀ 🖸 🅿 SB 🗲 🍴 ⚓	🛏 65.00 — 🛁 81.00 —	
Baywood Guest House, 98 Weston Road, **Aston Clinton**, Aylesbury, HP22 5EJ ☎ (0296) 630612		4🛏 3🛁 4🚿 🗑 🅿	🛏 12.50 16.00 🛁 25.00 30.00	
The Bell Inn, **Aston Clinton**, HP22 5HP ☎ (0296) 630252		21🛁 21🚿 ♿ 🗑 ♀ 🖸 🅿 🗲 🍴 ⚓	🛏 76.00 95.00 🛁 90.00 150.00	
West Lodge Hotel, 45 London Road, **Aston Clinton**, HP22 5HL ☎ (0296) 630331		2🛏 5🛁 7🚿 🗑 ♀ 🖸 🅿 ⚓	🛏 25.00 33.00 🛁 38.00 43.00	
The Bell, Market Square, **Aylesbury**, HP20 1TX ☎ (0296) 89835 & 82141		6🛏 11🛁 17🚿 🗑 ♀ 🖸 SB 🗲	🛏 56.00 57.00 🛁 67.00 68.00	
Forte Hotel, Aston Clinton Road, **Aylesbury**, HP22 5AA ☎ (0296) 393388		93🛁 7🅵 100🚿 ♿ 🗑 ♀ 🖸 🅿 SB 🗲 ⊕ ⚓	🛏 75.00 150.00 🛁 91.00 150.00	

Establishment Name & Address	Crown Classification	Bedroom Numbers and Facilities	Prices (£) MIN MAX
Hartwell House, Oxford Road, **Aylesbury**, HP17 8NL ☎ (0296) 747444	👑👑👑👑👑	5🛏 27🛏 32⊞ ♿ ᕗ8 ⬝ ⊞ 🅿 SB ⬝ ⬝ ⬝ ⬝	🛏 89.50 171.50 ⬝ 128.00 269.00
Horse and Jockey Motel, Buckingham Road, **Aylesbury**, HP19 3QL ☎ (0296) 23803	👑👑👑	24🛏 24⊞ ᕗ ⬝ ⊞ 🅿 SB ⬝ ⬝	🛏 23.00 35.00 ⬝ 33.00 45.00
The Wheatsheaf, Weedon, Nr. **Aylesbury**, HP22 4NS ☎ (0296) 641581	🅛	3🛏 5🛏 2⊞ ᕗ ⬝ 🅿 ⬝ ⬝ ⬝ ⬝	🛏 25.00 35.00 ⬝ 35.00 70.00
Bellhouse Hotel, Oxford Road, **Beaconsfield**, HP9 2XE ☎ (0753) 887211		20🛏 106🛏 10⊡ 136⊞ ♿ ᕗ ⬝ ⊞ 🅿 SB ⬝ ⬝	🛏 35.00 102.00 ⬝ 92.00 150.00
Chequers Hotel, Kiln Lane, Wooburn Common, Nr. **Beaconsfield**, HP10 0JQ ☎ (06285) 29575		16🛏 1⊡ 17⊞ ᕗ ⬝ ⊞ 🅿 SB ⬝ ⬝ ⬝ ⬝	🛏 64.00 — ⬝ 70.40 82.50
St. George's Wing, Priory Ford, Abbotsbrook, **Bourne End**, SL8 5QZ ☎ (06285) 20433	👑👑	1🛏 4🛏 1⊞ 🅿 ⬝	🛏 34.84 60.95 ⬝ 53.01 77.62
The White Hart, Market Square, **Buckingham**, MK18 1NL ☎ (0280) 815151		1🛏 17🛏 1⊡ 19⊞ ᕗ ⬝ ⊞ 🅿 SB ⬝ ⬝	🛏 54.00 — ⬝ 65.00 74.00
Burnham Beeches Hotel, Grove Road, **Burnham**, SL1 8DP ☎ (0628) 603333	👑👑👑	23🛏 56🛏 1⊡ 80⊞ ᕗ ⬝ ⊞ 🅿 SB ⬝ ⬝ ⬝ ⬝ ⬝	🛏 80.00 85.00 ⬝ 95.00 100.00
Milford Leys Farm, **Castlethorpe**, Milton Keynes, MK19 7HH ☎ (0908) 510153		2🛏 1⊡ ᕗ 🅿	🛏 12.50 14.00 ⬝ 22.00 25.00
Wallace Farm, **Dinton**, Nr. Aylesbury, HP17 8UF ☎ (0296) 748660	👑👑	2🛏 1⊡ 1⊞ ᕗ 🅿 ⬝	🛏 18.00 25.00 ⬝ 24.00 28.00
Bull Hotel, Oxford Road, **Gerrards Cross**, SL9 7PA ☎ (0753) 885995		13🛏 80🛏 2⊡ 95⊞ ♿ ᕗ ⬝ ⊞ 🅿 SB ⬝ ⬝ ⬝	🛏 77.00 77.00 ⬝ 97.00 130.00
Ethorpe Hotel, Packhorse Road, **Gerrards Cross**, SL9 8HY ☎ (0753) 882039	👑👑	4🛏 21🛏 4⊡ 29⊞ ♿ ᕗ ⬝ ⊞ 🅿 SB ⬝ ⬝	🛏 62.00 62.00 ⬝ 72.50 72.50
Mr. & Mrs. I. Lee-Duncan, 1 White House Close, Chalfont St. Peter, **Gerrards Cross**, SL9 0DA ☎ (0753) 885401	🅛	1🛏 1⊞ 🅿	🛏 — 20.00 ⬝ — 35.00
Hatton Court Hotel and Restaurant, Burlington End, **Hanslope**, Milton Keynes, MK19 7BQ ☎ (0908) 510044		6🛏 6⊡ 12⊞ ᕗ3 ⬝ ⊞ 🅿 SB ⬝ ⬝	🛏 40.00 80.00 ⬝ 80.00 110.00

Establishment Name & Address	Crown Classification	Bedroom Numbers and Facilities	Prices (£) MIN	MAX
Crest Hotel, Crest Road, Handycross, **High Wycombe**, HP11 1TL ☎ (0494) 442100		24🛏 87⚄ 111⊞ ♿ ⇘ ⬚ 🅿 SB ⌁	89.00 109.00	— —
The Fox Country Hotel, Ibstone, **High Wycombe**, HP14 3GG ☎ (049163) 289 & 722	👑👑👑👑	8⚄ 1🄵 9⊞ ⇘ ⬚ 🅿 SB ⌁ ♨	30.00 48.00	48.00 60.00
Old Jordans, Jordans Lane, **Jordans**, Nr. Beaconsfield, HP9 2SW ☎ (02407) 4586		16🛏 13⚄ 2🄵 9⊞ ⇘ 🅿 SB ⌁ ♨ ⌁	21.50 36.00	32.50 50.00
The Compleat Angler, Bisham Road, Marlow Bridge, **Marlow**, SL7 1RG ☎ (06284) 4444		9🛏 37⚄ 46⊞ ⇘ ⬚ 🅿 SB ⌁ ♨ ✆ ⌁	94.00 117.00	107.00 127.00
The Country House, Bisham, **Marlow**, SL7 1RP ☎ (0628) 890606	👑👑👑👑	3🛏 3⚄ 1🄵 7⊞ ♿ ⇘ ⬚ 🅿	48.00 65.00	— —
New Road Bed & Breakfast, 50A New Road, Marlow Bottom, **Nr. Marlow**, SL7 3NW ☎ (06284) 72666		2🛏 1⚄ ⇘ 🅿	13.00 26.00	15.00 30.00
Danesfield House, Medmenham Marlow SL7 3ES ☎ Tel No. (0628) 891010		95-Bedroom exclusive hotel with conference facilities and choice of restaurants open Spring 1990	— —	— —
Broughton Hotel, Broughton Village, **Nr Milton Keynes**, MK10 9AA ☎ (0908) 667726	👑👑👑👑	28⚄ 2🄵 30⊞ ♿ ⇘ ⬚ 🅿 SB ⌁	49.50 59.50	59.50 69.50
The Bull Hotel, 64 High Street, Stony Stratford, **Milton Keynes**, MK11 1AQ ☎ (0908) 567104	🄻	2🛏 11⚄ 1🄵 14⊞ ⇘5 ⬚ 🅿 SB ♨ ⌁	33.00 43.00	33.00 43.00
Friendly Lodge, Monks Way, Two Mile Ash, **Milton Keynes**, MK8 8LY ☎ (0908) 561666		45⚄ 5🄵 50⊞ ♿ ⇘ ⬚ 🅿 SB ♨ ⌁	45.50 61.00	50.00 66.00
Haversham Grange, Haversham, **Milton Keynes**, MK19 7DX ☎ (0908) 312389	🄻	3⚄ 2⊞ ⇘5 🅿 ♨ ✆	18.00 35.00	20.00 40.00
Post House Hotel, 500 Saxon Gate West, Central **Milton Keynes**, MK9 2HQ ☎ (0908) 667722		12🛏 151⚄ 163⊞ ♿ ⇘ ⬚ 🅿 SB ⌁ ✆ ⌁	72.00 83.00	85.00 100.00
Vignoble, 2 Medland, Woughton Park, **Milton Keynes**, MK6 3BH ☎ (0908) 666804	🄻	1🛏 2⚄ ⇘5 🅿	14.50 28.00	16.00 31.00
The Wayfarer Hotel, Brickhill Street, Willen Lake, **Milton Keynes** MK15 0DS ☎ (0908) 675222		11🛏 30⚄ 41⊞ ⇘ ⬚ 🅿 SB ✆ ⌁	32.50 39.50	52.00 49.50

Establishment Name & Address	Crown Classification	Bedroom Numbers and Facilities	Prices (£) MIN MAX
Holywell Farm, Thornton Road, Nash, **Milton Keynes**, MK17 0EY ☎ (0908) 501769	♛ ♛ ♛	4🛏 2⊡ ⇘ ⊞	20.00 — 30.00 —
Woughton House Hotel, Woughton-on-the-Green, **Milton Keynes**, MK6 3LR ☎ (0908) 661919		7🛏 11🛏 2⊡ 20⊡ ⇘ ⛾ ⊞ ⊞ SB ⚶ ⚑	35.50 57.50 42.00 62.50
Coach House Hotel, London Road, Maulsoe, **Newport Pagnell**, MK16 0JA ☎ (0742) 620180 – Regional Office		49-Bedroom hotel with conference facilities to open February 1990	— — — —
Swan Revived Hotel, High Street, **Newport Pagnell**, Milton Keynes, MK16 8AR ☎ (0908) 610565	♛ ♛ ♛ ♛	20🛏 19🛏 2⊡ 41⊡ ♿ ⇘ ⛾ ⊞ ⊞ SB ⊞ ⊞ ⚑	20.00 46.00 32.00 50.00
Thurstons Private Hotel, 90 High Street, **Newport Pagnell**, Milton Keynes, MK16 8EH ☎ (0908) 611377	🅛	5🛏 4🛏 9⊡ ♿ ⇘ ⊞ ⊞ SB	20.00 35.00 30.00 45.00
Welcome Lodge, M1 Motorway Service Area No 3, **Newport Pagnell**, MK16 8DS ☎ (0908) 610878		95🛏 2⊡ 97⊡ ♿ ⇘ ⛾ ⊞ ⊞ SB ⚶ ⚑	42.50 — 52.50 —
Shoulder of Mutton Inn, **Owlswick**, Aylesbury, HP17 9RH ☎ (08444) 4304	♛ ♛ ♛ ♛	16🛏 1⊡ 17⊡ ♿ ⇘ ⛾ ⊞ ⊞ SB ⊞ ⚑	34.00 36.00 44.00 52.00
The Rose & Crown Inn, Wycombe Road, **Saunderton**, Nr. Princes Risborough, HP17 9NP ☎ (08444) 5299	♛ ♛ ♛	6🛏 11🛏 14⊡ ⇘5 ⛾ ⊞ ⊞ SB ⚑	35.00 64.00 54.00 75.00
Cliveden, **Taplow**, SL6 0JF ☎ (06286) 68561 For details see page 36	♛ ♛ ♛ ♛ ♛	3🛏 28🛏 31⊡ ⇘ ⛾ ⊞ ⊞ ⚶ ⊞ ⊞ ✚ ⚑	130.00 — 170.00 —
George & Dragon Hotel, **West Wycombe**, HP14 3AB ☎ (0494) 464414		1🛏 8🛏 1⊡ 10⊡ ⇘ ⛾ ⊞ ⊞ SB ⊞ ⊞ ⚑	36.00 39.00 46.00 49.00
The Priory Hotel, 70–72 High Street, **Whitchurch**, Nr. Aylesbury, HP22 4JS ☎ (0296) 641239	♛ ♛ ♛ ♛	3🛏 7🛏 1⊡ 1⊡ ⇘ ⛾ ⊞ ⊞ ⊞ ⊞ ⚑	51.75 55.20 74.75 80.50
Bell Hotel, Market Square, **Winslow**, MK18 3AB ☎ (029671) 2741	♛ ♛ ♛ ♛	4🛏 9🛏 2⊡ 13⊡ ⇘ ⛾ ⊞ ⊞ SB ⊞ ⚑	45.00 55.00 50.00 60.00

Hertfordshire

Establishment Name & Address	Crown Classification	Bedroom Numbers and Facilities	Prices (£) MIN	MAX
Pennyfarthing House, 296–298 High Street, **Berkhamsted**, HP4 1AJ ☎ (0442) 872828		12🛏 12🚿 ⓢ Ⓨ 💷 🅿 SB 🎱 🏮 ⓣ	40.00 45.00	60.00 65.00
Bedford Arms Thistle Hotel, **Chenies**, Rickmansworth, WD3 6EQ ☎ (09278) 3301	👑👑👑👑	3🛏 7🚾 10🚿 ⓢ Ⓨ 💷 🅿 SB 🏮 ⓣ	72.50 95.00	82.50 100.00
The Two Brewers, The Common, **Chipperfield**, Kings Langley, WD4 9BS ☎ (09277) 65266		20🚾 20🚿 ⓢ Ⓨ 💷 🅿 SB ⚲	68.00 79.00	— —
Edgwarebury Hotel, Barnet Lane, **Elstree**, WD6 3RE ☎ 01–953 8227	👑👑👑👑	20🛏 30🚾 50🚿 ⓢ Ⓨ 💷 🅿 SB ⚲ 🎱 🏮 ⊕ ⓣ	70.00 80.00	90.00 —
Glen Eagle Hotel, 1 Luton Road, **Harpenden**, AL5 2PX ☎ (05827) 60271		6🛏 39🚾 6🅵 51🚿 ⓢ Ⓨ 💷 🅿 SB ⚲ 🏮 ⓣ	59.50 72.00	— —
Harpenden Moat House Hotel, 18 Southdown Road, **Harpenden**, AL5 1PE ☎ (05827) 64111	👑👑👑👑👑	8🛏 35🚾 10🅵 53🚿 ⓢ Ⓨ 💷 🅿 SB 🎱 🏮 ⓣ	40.00 60.00	75.00 95.00
Milton Hotel, 25 Milton Road, **Harpenden**, AL5 5LA ☎ (05827) 62914	👑	5🛏 3🚾 3🚿 ⓢ Ⓨ 🅿 🏮 ⓣ	19.00 29.00	25.00 32.00
Comet Hotel, 301 St Albans Road West, **Hatfield**, AL10 9RH ☎ (0707) 265411	👑👑👑👑	19🛏 35🚾 3🅵 54🚿 ⓢ Ⓨ 💷 🅿 SB 🏮 ⓣ	64.50 81.00	74.50 91.00
Hatfield Lodge Hotel, Comet Way, **Hatfield**, AL10 9NG ☎ (0707) 272661		17🛏 3🚾 20🚿 ⓢ Ⓨ 💷 🅿 ⓣ	52.50 67.50	— —
Hatfield Polytechnic and Conference Service, College Lane, **Hatfield**, AL10 9AB ☎ (0707) 27631		6🛏 ♿ ⓢ5 🅿	14.50 —	14.50 —
Hazel Grove Hotel, Roehyde Way, **Hatfield**, AL10 9AF ☎ (07072) 75701 (6 lines)		28🚾 28🚿 ♿ ⓢ Ⓨ 💷 🅿 SB ⚲ ⓣ	60.00 68.00	68.00 90.00
Midland Hotel, Midland Road, **Hemel Hempstead**, HP2 5BH ☎ (0442) 53218	🅛	3🛏 3🚾 6🚿 ⓢ Ⓨ 💷 🅿 SB 🎱 🏮	38.50 50.00	38.50 50.00
Post House Hotel, Breakspear Way, **Hemel Hempstead**, HP2 4UA ☎ (0442) 51122		29🛏 70🚾 8🅵 107🚿 ⓢ Ⓨ 💷 🅿 SB ⚲ ⓣ	36.00 75.00	72.00 83.00

99

Establishment Name & Address	Crown Classification	Bedroom Numbers and Facilities	Prices (£) MIN	MAX
The Cowper Arms, Cole Green Lane, Letty Green, **Hertford**, SG14 2NN ☎ (0707) 330202		2🛏 3🛏 ⑤ ⑨ ⊞ ℗ SB ⚲ 🏠	40.00 51.00	40.00 51.00
The White Horse, Hertingfordbury, **Hertford**, SG14 2LB ☎ (0992) 586791		19🛏 16🛏 7🅵 42⊞ ⑤ ⑨ ⊞ ℗ SB ⚲ 🍴	62.00 82.00	73.00 82.00
Avenue Guesthouse, 2 The Avenue, Highbury, **Hitchin**, SG4 9RG ☎ (0462) 35508		1🛏 1🛏 1🅵 ⑤6 ℗	11.00 20.00	15.00 25.00
Blakemore Thistle Hotel, **Little Wymondley** Nr. Hitchin, SG4 7JJ ☎ (0438) 355821	♔ ♔ ♔ ♔	6🛏 74🛏 2🅵 82⊞ ♿ ⑤ ⑨ ⊞ ℗ SB ⚲ 🍴	56.25 69.50	71.25 89.50
The Lord Lister Hotel, Park Street, **Hitchin**, SG4 9AH ☎ (0462) 32712 & 59451	Ⓛ	6🛏 14🛏 1🅵 10⊞ ⑤ ⑨ ⊞ ℗ SB 🏠 🍴	25.00 38.00	38.00 48.00
Redcoats Farmhouse Hotel, Redcoats Green, Nr. **Hitchin**, SG4 7JR ☎ (0438) 729500	♚ ♚ ♚	1🛏 11🛏 2🅵 11⊞ ⑤ ⑨ ⊞ ℗ SB 🏠 🍴	30.00 42.00	49.00 65.00
Greenlawns Hotel, Sollershott East, **Letchworth**, SG6 3JW ☎ (0462) 683143		11🛏 2🛏 ⑤ ⑨ ⊞ ℗ 🍴	25.00 38.00	— —
Vintage Corner Hotel, Old Cambridge Road, **Puckeridge**, SG11 1SA ☎ (0920) 822722	Ⓛ	42🛏 42⊞ ⑤ ⑨ ⊞ ℗ ⊙ 🍴	38.50 48.50	58.50 68.50
Aubrey Park Hotel, Hemel Hempstead Road, **Redbourn**, Nr. St. Albans, AL3 7AF ☎ (058285) 2105	♚ ♚ ♚ ♚	23🛏 76🛏 3🅵 102⊞ ♿ ⑤ ⑨ ⊞ ℗ SB 🏠 🍴	75.00 90.00	85.00 100.00
The Apples Hotel, 133 London Road, **St. Albans**, AL1 1TA ☎ (0727) 44111	♚ ♚ ♚ ♚	1🛏 4🛏 5⊞ ⑤ ⑨ ⊞ ℗	30.00 63.00	55.00 70.00
The Care Inn, 29 Alma Road, **St. Albans**, AL1 3AT ☎ (0727) 67310	♚ ♚	1🛏 1🛏 1🅵 1⊞ ⑤ ℗ SB 🏠 ⊙	15.00 26.00	18.00 30.00
Hertfordshire Moat House Hotel, London Road, Flamstead, Markyate, **St. Albans**, AL3 8HH ☎ (0582) 840840	♚ ♚ ♚ ♚	95🛏 95⊞ ⑤ ⑨ ⊞ ℗ SB ⚲ 🏠 🍴	40.00 —	72.00 —
Lake Holidays Hotel, 234 London Road, **St. Albans**, AL1 1JQ ☎ (0727) 40904	♚ ♚ ♚ ♚	19🛏 21🛏 2🅵 42⊞ ♿ ⑤ ⑨ ⊞ ℗ SB ⚲ 🏠 🍴	36.50 54.50	59.90 86.30

Establishment Name & Address	Crown Classification	Bedroom Numbers and Facilities	Prices (£) MIN	MAX
Newpark House Hotel, North Orbital Road, Nr. London Colney Roundabout, **St. Albans**, AL1 1EG ☎ (0727) 24839	L	10 4	18.00 36.00	21.00 42.00
The Noke Thistle Hotel, Watford Road, **St Albans**, AL2 3DS ☎ (0727) 54252	👑👑👑👑	52 5 57	77.25 94.50	82.25 99.50
St Michael's Manor Hotel, Fishpool Street, **St. Albans**, AL3 4RY ☎ (0727) 64444	👑👑👑👑	11 15 26	52.00 60.00	68.00 85.00
Sopwell House, Cottonmill Lane, Sopwell, **St. Albans**, AL1 2HQ ☎ (0727) 64477	👑👑👑👑👑	11 59 70	67.50 90.25	78.50 97.25
Crest Hotel, (M25 junction 23), **South Mimms**, Potters Bar, EN6 3NH ☎ (0707) 43311		125 125	86.00 100.00	90.00 110.00
Archways Hotel, 11, 15, 21 Hitchin Road, **Stevenage**, SG1 2BH ☎ (0438) 316640		8 25 2 35	32.00 37.00	43.50 48.50
Novotel, Knebworth Park, **Stevenage**, SG1 2AX ☎ (0438) 742299		101 101	65.00 73.75	67.00 75.00
The Roebuck, Old London Road, Broadwater, **Stevenage**, SG2 8DS ☎ (0438) 365444		18 36 54	40.00 50.00	67.00 78.00
The Rose & Crown, High Street, **Tring**, HP23 5AH ☎ (044282) 4071	👑👑👑👑	7 20 1 28	60.00 70.00	— —
The Royal Hotel, Station Approach, Tring Station, **Tring**, HP23 5QR ☎ (044282) 7616	👑👑👑	3 13 2 15	38.00 44.00	48.00 48.00
Briggens House Hotel, Stanstead Road, Stanstead Abbotts, Nr. **Ware**, SG12 8LD ☎ (027979) 2416	👑👑👑👑	15 39 54	80.00 110.00	102.00 148.50
Feathers Inn, Wadesmill, Nr. **Ware**, SG12 0TN ☎ (0920) 46206		9 13 15	44.00 54.50	48.00 58.50
Hanbury Manor, Thundridge, **Ware**, SG12 0SD ☎ (0992) 500565		1 97 98	125.00 135.00	— 175.00
Ware Moat House, Baldock Street, **Ware**, SG12 9DR ☎ (0920) 465011		6 44 50	22.25 44.50	62.50 72.50

Establishment Name & Address	Crown Classification	Bedroom Numbers and Facilities	Prices (£) MIN MAX
Dean Park Hotel, 30/40 St. Albans Road, **Watford**, WD1 1RN ☎ (0923) 229212		40🛏 50♨ 90⊞ 🛬 ♀ 🖭 🅿 SB ⟟	⤇ 65.00 85.00 ♨ — —
Hilton National Watford, Elton Way, **Watford**, WD2 8HA ☎ (0923) 35881		160♨ 3🄵 163⊞ ♿ 🛬12 ♀ 🖭 🅿 SB 🗲 ⟟	⤇ 75.00 90.00 ♨ 90.00 105.00
Spiders Web Hotel, Watford by-Pass (A41), **Watford**, WD2 8HQ ☎ (01-) 950 6211	♛ ♛ ♛ ♛ ♛	7🛏 153♨ 10🄵 170⊞ 🛬 ♀ 🖭 🅿 SB 🗲 ✪ ⟟	⤇ 40.00 70.00 ♨ 50.00 80.00
Heath Lodge Hotel, Danesbury Park Road, **Welwyn**, AL6 9SN ☎ (043871) 7064		8🛏 17♨ 22🄵 47⊞ ♿ ♀ 🖭 🅿 SB 🗲 ⟟	⤇ 65.00 150.00 ♨ 80.00 250.00
Tewin Bury Farmhouse, Tewin Bury Farm, Nr. **Welwyn**, AL6 0JB (043871) 7793	♛ ♛ ♛	2🛏 2♨ 4⊞ 🛬9 🖭 🅿 SB 🐾 ⟟	⤇ 25.00 40.00 ♨ 46.00 59.50
Crest Hotel, Homestead Court, **Welwyn Garden City**, AL7 4LX ☎ (0707) 324336		58♨ 58⊞ ♿ 🛬1 ♀ 🖭 🅿 SB 🗲 ⟟	⤇ 78.00 — ♨ 98.00 —

Oxfordshire

Abingdon Lodge Hotel, Marcham Road, **Abingdon**, OX14 1TZ ☎ (0235) 553456	♛ ♛ ♛ ♛ ♛	63♨ 63⊞ 🛬 ♀ 🖭 🅿 SB ⟟	⤇ 38.00 62.00 ♨ 44.00 70.00
Crown and Thistle Hotel, Bridge Street, **Abingdon**, OX14 3HS ☎ (0235) 22556	♛ ♛	5🛏 14♨ 2🄵 21⊞ 🛬 ♀ 🖭 🅿 SB 🐾 🛏 ⟟	⤇ 37.50 42.50 ♨ — —
Dog House Hotel, Frilford Heath, **Abingdon**, OX13 6QJ ☎ (0865) 390830		1🛏 15♨ 3🄵 19⊞ ♿ 🛬 ♀ 🖭 🅿 SB 🛏 🗲 ⟟	⤇ 39.50 — ♨ 52.50 —
Thame Lane House, 1 Thame Lane, Culham, **Abingdon**, OX14 3DS ☎ (0235) 24177	♛	3🛏 1♨ 1🄵 1⊞ 🛬3 ♀ 🅿	⤇ 19.00 25.00 ♨ 34.00 40.00
The Upper Reaches, Thames Street, **Abingdon**, OX14 3JA ☎ (0235) 22311		6🛏 20♨ 26⊞ 🛬 ♀ 🖭 🅿 SB 🐾 🛏 ⟟	⤇ 60.00 68.00 ♨ 75.00 82.00
Mr. Warrick's Arms Hotel, Ock Street, **Abingdon**, OX14 5DQ ☎ (0235) 22470 & 22974		2🛏 8♨ 6⊞ 🛬 ♀ 🅿 🛏	⤇ 16.00 17.00 ♨ 30.00 36.00
Rose & Crown Hotel, **Ashbury**, Swindon, SN6 8NA ☎ (079371) 222		11♨ 1⊞ 🛬 ♀ 🖭 🅿 SB 🛏 🗲 ⟟	⤇ 23.00 — ♨ 36.00 —

Establishment Name & Address	Crown Classification	Bedroom Numbers and Facilities	Prices (£) MIN MAX	
Farmhouse Hotel and Restaurant, University Farm, Lew, **Bampton**, OX8 2AU ☎ (0993) 850297 & 851480	♕♕♕♕	4🛏 2🅕 6⊞ ♿ ⇖8 ⬤ 🅿 SB 🏠 🌙 ⛵	⇔ 25.00 — ⇔ 37.00 —
Morar Farmhouse, Weald Street, **Bampton**, OX8 2HL ☎ (0993) 850162	♕♕	3🛏 ⇖6 ⬤ 🅿 SB 🌙	⇔ 16.50 19.50 ⇔ 25.00 28.00
Banbury Moat House, Oxford Road, **Banbury**, OX16 9AH ☎ (0295) 59361		11🛏 36🛏 1🅕 48⊞ ⇖ ⬤ 🅿 SB 🏠 🌙 ⛵	⇔ 21.00 59.00 ⇔ 42.00 69.00
Cromwell Lodge Hotel, North Bar, **Banbury**, OX16 0TB ☎ (0295) 59781	♕♕♕♕	13🛏 17🛏 2🅕 32⊞ ⇖ ⬤ ⊞ 🅿 SB 🌙 ⛵	⇔ 41.00 53.00 ⇔ 52.00 65.00
Easington House Hotel, 50 Oxford Road, **Banbury**, OX16 9AN ☎ (0295) 59395	♕♕♕♕	2🛏 6🛏 4🅕 9⊞ ♿ ⇖ ⬤ ⊞ 🅿 SB 🏠 🌙 ⛵	⇔ 20.00 56.00 ⇔ 45.00 70.00
Fernleigh Guesthouse, 67 Oxford Road, **Banbury**, OX16 9AJ ☎ (0295) 50645		2🛏 3🛏 3🅕 1⊞ ⇖2 🅿 SB ⛵	⇔ 18.00 32.00 ⇔ 33.00 40.00
Lismore Hotel and Restaurant, 61 Oxford Road, **Banbury**, OX16 9AJ ☎ (0295) 67661	♕♕♕♕	10🛏 7🛏 4🅕 18⊞ ♿ ⇖ ⬤ ⊞ 🅿 SB ⋇ 🌙 ⛵	⇔ 25.00 40.00 ⇔ 50.00 50.00
Prospect House Guest House, 70 Oxford Road, **Banbury**, OX16 9AN ☎ (0295) 268749	♕♕♕	1🛏 7🛏 8⊞ ⇖ ⊞ 🅿 SB	⇔ 23.00 28.00 ⇔ 34.00 38.00
Swalcliffe Manor, Swalcliffe, Nr. **Banbury**, OX15 5EH ☎ (029578) 348		3🛏 2⊞ 🅿 🏠 🌙 ◉ ⛵	⇔ — — ⇔ 30.00 50.00
Tredis Guest House, 15 Broughton Road, **Banbury**, OX16 9QB ☎ (0295) 4632	♕♕	5🛏 5🛏 1🅕 2⊞ ⇖ 🅿 ⛵	⇔ 15.00 20.00 ⇔ 28.00 35.00
Whately Hall, Horsefair, Banbury Cross, **Banbury**, OX16 0AN ☎ (0295) 263451		18🛏 56🛏 74⊞ ⇖ ⬤ ⊞ 🅿 SB ⋇ 🏠 ⛵	⇔ 72.00 78.00 ⇔ 80.00 91.90
Wroxton House Hotel, Wroxton St. Mary, Nr. **Banbury**, OX15 6QB ☎ (0295) 730482	♕♕♕♕	7🛏 26🛏 1🅕 34⊞ ⇖ ⬤ ⊞ 🅿 SB ⋇ 🏠 🌙 ◉ ⛵	⇔ 70.00 75.00 ⇔ 90.00 100.00
Kings Arms Hotel, Market Square, **Bicester**, OX6 7AH ☎ (0869) 252015	♕	3🛏 15🛏 1🅕 19⊞ ⇖ ⬤ ⊞ 🌙 ⛵	⇔ 41.00 — ⇔ 51.00 —
Old School Hotel, Church Street, **Bloxham**, OX15 4ET ☎ (0295) 720369	♕♕♕♕	4🛏 32🛏 2🅕 38⊞ ♿ ⇖ ⬤ ⊞ 🅿 SB 🏠 🌙 ◉ ⛵	⇔ 48.00 48.00 ⇔ 60.00 75.00

103

Establishment Name & Address	Crown Classification	Bedroom Numbers and Facilities	Prices (£) MIN	MAX
Wall Tree House Farm, Steane, **Brackley**, NN13 5NS ☎ (0295) 811235		6♜ 2🄵 7🖭 ⟓ ⏛ 🛏 🅿 EM	⨟ 21.00 ⨟ 32.00	26.00 35.00
Bay Tree Hotel, Sheep Street, **Burford**, OX8 4LW ☎ (099382) 3137		2⨝ 18♜ 2🄵 22🖭 ⟓ ⏛ 🛏 🅿 SB ⚒ 🎠 🖾 ☏	⨟ 35.00 ⨟ 60.00	60.00 105.00
Bull Hotel, High Street, **Burford**, OX8 4RH ☎ (099382) 2220		2⨝ 11♜ 1🄵 10🖭 ⟓ ⏛ 🛏 🅿 SB ⚒ 🎠 🖾 ☏	⨟ 35.00 ⨟ 47.50	45.00 65.00
Cotswold Gateway Hotel, Cheltenham Road, **Burford**, OX9 4HX ☎ (099382) 3345 & 2695	♛ ♛ ♛ ♛	12♜ 5🄵 17🖭 ♿ ⟓ ⏛ 🛏 🅿 SB ⚒ ☏	⨟ 38.50 ⨟ 58.50	42.50 70.00
Elm Farm House, Meadow Lane, Fulbrook, **Burford**, OX8 4BW ☎ (099382) 3611/2	♛ ♛	1⨝ 6♜ 3🖭 ⟓10 ⏛ 🛏 🅿 SB	⨟ 22.00 ⨟ 30.00	26.00 42.00
Golden Pheasant Hotel, High Street, **Burford**, OX8 4RJ ☎ (099382) 3223 & 3417	♛ ♛ ♛ ♛	1⨝ 9♜ 2🄵 12🖭 ♿ ⟓ ⏛ 🛏 🅿 SB ⚒ 🎠 🖾 ☏	⨟ 39.00 ⨟ 57.00	45.00 78.00
The Highway Hotel, High Street, **Burford**, OX8 4RG ☎ (099382) 2136	♛ ♛ ♛ ♛	9♜ 1🄵 8🖭 ⟓ ⏛ SB ⚒ 🎠 🖾	⨟ 30.00 ⨟ 50.00	35.00 55.00
The Inn for All Seasons, The Barringtons, **Burford**, OX8 4TN ☎ (04514) 324		10♜ 10🖭 ⟓10 ⏛ 🛏 🅿 SB ⚒ 🎠 ☏	⨟ 31.50 ⨟ 49.00	37.50 65.00
The Lamb Inn, Sheep Street, **Burford**, Oxon, OX8 4LR ☎ (099382) 3155	♛ ♛ ♛	3⨝ 11♜ 8🖭 ⟓ ⏛ 🅿 SB ⚒ 🎠 🖾 ☏	⨟ 30.00 ⨟ 50.00	35.00 64.00
The Maytime Inn, Asthall, **Burford**, OX8 4HW ☎ (000382) 2068	♛ ♛	6♜ 6🖭 ♿ ⟓ ⏛ 🛏 🅿 🎠 ☏	⨟ 35.00 ⨟ 47.50	— —
Burleigh Farm, **Cassington**, OX8 1EA ☎ (0865) 881352		1⨝ 1♜ 1🄵 2🖭 ⟓ 🅿 🎠	⨟ ⨟ 27.00	— —
Chadlington House Hotel, **Chadlington**, OX7 3LZ ☎ (060876) 437		2⨝ 9♜ 1🄵 11🖭 ⟓8 ⏛ 🅿 SB 🎠 🖾 ☏	⨟ 29.50 ⨟ 25.00	35.00 40.00
The Bell Hotel, Church Street, **Charlbury**, OX7 3AP ☎ (0608) 810278	♛ ♛ ♛ ♛	2⨝ 11♜ 1🄵 14🖭 ♿ ⟓ ⏛ 🅿 SB ⚒ 🎠 ☏	⨟ 45.00 ⨟ 60.00	55.00 70.00
Crowell End, Spriggs Alley, Crowell Hill, Nr. **Chinnor**, OX9 4BT ☎ (0844) 52726		1⨝ 2♜ 1🖭 ⟓ 🅿	⨟ 12.50 ⨟ 30.00	12.50 30.00

Establishment Name & Address	Crown Classification	Bedroom Numbers and Facilities	Prices (£) MIN MAX
Plough and Harrow, Sydenham, **Chinnor**, OX9 4LD ☎ (0844) 51367	⚜⚜⚜⚜	2⇋ 5⚏ 7⊞ ♀ ⌸ 🅿 SB ⚲ ⌨	20.00 45.00 / 35.00 60.00
The Crown & Cushion Hotel, 23 High Street, **Chipping Norton**, OX7 5AD ☎ (0608) 2533	⚜⚜⚜⚜	6⇋ 11⚏ 1⒡ 18⊞ ⛵♀⌸🅿 SB ⚲ ⌂ ⌨ ⵁ	29.50 35.00 / 43.00 59.00
The Forge Guest House, The Forge House, Churchill, Nr. **Chipping Norton**, OX7 6NJ ☎ (060871) 8173	⚜⚜⚜	4⚏ 1⒡ 5⊞ ⛵♀ SB ⚲ ⌂ ⌨ ✪	20.00 45.00 / 30.00 45.00
Market House, 4 Middle Row, **Chipping Norton**, OX7 5NH ☎ (0608) 2781	⚜⚜	3⚏ 3⊞ ⛵♀⌸🅿 SB	16.00 17.50 / 32.00 35.00
The White Hart, High Street, **Chipping Norton**, OX7 5AD ☎ (0608) 2572		4⇋ 15⚏ 2⒡ ⛵♀⌸🅿 SB ⚲ ⌂ ⌨ ⵁ	39.50 42.00 / 63.50 95.00
The Coach and Horses, Stadhampton Road, **Chislehampton**, OX9 7UX ☎ (0865) 890255	⚜⚜	9⚏ 9⊞ ♿ ⛵5 ♀⌸🅿 ⌂	33.00 48.50 / 45.00 65.00
Plough Hotel & Restaurant, **Clanfield**, Oxford, OX8 2RB ☎ (036781) 222 & 494	⚜⚜	6⚏ 6⊞ ⛵♀⌸🅿 SB ⚲ ⌂ ⌨ ⵁ	65.00 80.00 / 75.00 115.00
The Barley Mow Hotel, **Clifton Hampden**, Abingdon, OX14 3EH ☎ (086730) 7847		2⇋ 2⚏ 1⊞ ⛵♀⌸🅿 SB ⌂	31.00 31.00 / 49.00 49.00
Holcombe Hotel & Restaurant, High Street, **Deddington**, OX5 4SL ☎ (0869) 38274	⚜⚜⚜⚜	2⇋ 11⚏ 1⒡ 14⊞ ⛵♀⌸🅿 SB ⚲ ⌂ ⵁ	49.50 65.00 / 59.50 78.00
The George Hotel, High Street, **Dorchester-on-Thames**, OX9 8HH ☎ (0865) 340404	🅛	3⇋ 12⚏ 2⒡ 17⊞ ⛵10 ♀⌸🅿 SB ⌂ ⌨ ⵁ	48.00 58.00 / 67.00 105.00
White Hart Hotel, High Street, **Dorchester-on-Thames**, OX9 8HN ☎ (0865) 340074	⚜⚜⚜⚜	2⇋ 16⚏ 2⒡ 20⊞ ♿⛵♀⌸🅿 SB ⌨ ⵁ	52.00 57.20 / 72.00 79.20
The Ridgeway Lodge, Skeats Bush, **East Hendred**, OX12 8LH ☎ (0235) 833360	⚜⚜	4⇋ 12⚏ 4⒡ 9⊞ ⛵♀⌸🅿 SB ⚲	16.00 — / 34.00 —
The Apple Tree Inn, Buscot, **Faringdon**, SN7 8DA ☎ (0367) 52592		3⚏ ⛵♀🅿 SB ⌂ ⌨	20.00 — / 27.00 —
Bowling Green Farm, Stanford Road, **Faringdon**, SN7 8EZ ☎ (0367) 20229/240229	⚜⚜⚜	2⒡ 2⊞ ⛵🅿 SB	18.00 — / 28.00 —

105

Establishment Name & Address	Crown Classification	Bedroom Numbers and Facilities	Prices (£) MIN	MAX
The Crown Hotel, Market Place, **Faringdon**, SN7 7HU ☎ (0367) 22744 (Spring 1990)		2⇔ 9♨ 1🛏 8⊞ ⟿ ⬭ 🖭 🅿 SB 🍴 🚪 ♟	32.00 39.00	40.00 46.00
Faringdon Hotel, Market Place, **Faringdon**, SN7 7HL ☎ (0367) 20536	👑👑👑👑	6⇔ 13♨ 3🛏 22⊞ ⟿ ⬭ 🅿 🚪 ♟	36.00 46.00	38.00 48.00
Portwell Guest House, Market Place, **Faringdon**, SN7 7HU ☎ (0367) 20197	👑👑👑	1⇔ 4♨ 2🛏 7⊞ ⟿ ⬭ 🅿 SB 🍴	24.00 31.00	24.00 31.00
Stroud Court Hotel, Oxford Road, **Farmoor**, OX2 9NN ☎ (0865) 883311 & 881820		4⇔ 13♨ 2⊞ Opening April 1990	— —	— —
The Hunter's Lodge, Stow Road, **Fifield**, OX7 6HR ☎ (0993) 831652	👑👑	11♨ 2🛏 12⊞ ⟿ ⬭ 🅿 SB 🍴	— 45.00	— —
Little Parmoor, **Frieth**, Nr. Henley on Thames, RG9 6NL ☎ (0494) 881447	Ⓛ	1⇔ 2♨ ⟿9 🅿 🍴	15.00 30.00	15.00 30.00
The Ark, Wantage Road, **Frilford**, Nr. Abingdon, OX13 5NZ ☎ (0865) 391911/391470	👑👑	6♨ 6⊞ ♿ ⟿ ⬭ 🅿 SB 🍴 ♟	35.00 45.00	45.00 55.00
Manor Farm, **Fyfield**, Abingdon, OX13 5LR ☎ (0865) 390485	Ⓛ	2🛏 ⟿ 🅿 🍴 ⊕	— —	12.00 22.00
Le Manoir aux Quat' Saisons, Church Road, **Great Milton**, OX9 7PD ☎ (0844) 278881	👑👑👑👑👑	21♨ 21⊞ ♿ ⟿ ⬭ 🖭 🅿 SB 🍴 🚪 ⊕ ♟	— 150.00	— 300.00
Kingswell Hotel and Restaurant, Reading Road, **Harwell**, Nr. Didcot, OX11 0LZ ☎ (0235) 833043		19♨ 19⊞ ♿ ⟿ ⬭ 🅿 SB 🍴 ♟	55.00 75.00	— —
The Edwardian Hotel, Station Road, **Henley-on-Thames**, RG9 1AT ☎ (0491) 578678	👑👑👑	9⇔ 7♨ 2🛏 18⊞ ⟿ ⬭ 🖭 🅿 SB 🌿 🍴 🚪 ♟	52.50 62.50	— —
Flohrs Hotel and Restaurant, 15 Northfield End, **Henley-on-Thames**, RG9 2JG ☎ (0491) 573412	👑👑👑	3⇔ 2♨ 4🛏 4⊞ ⟿ ⬭ 🅿 🍴 ♟	31.00 49.00	53.00 74.00
Phyllis Court Club, Marlow Road, **Henley-on-Thames**, RG9 2HT ☎ (0491) 574366		1⇔ 8♨ 9⊞ ⬭ 🖭 🅿 🍴 ♟	60.00 80.00	80.00 90.00
Red Lion Hotel, Thameside, **Henley-on-Thames**, RG9 2AR ☎ (0491) 572161		5⇔ 20♨ 1🛏 22⊞ ⟿ ⬭ 🖭 🅿 SB 🌿 🍴 🚪 ♟	50.00 80.00	70.00 95.00

Establishment Name & Address	Crown Classification	Bedroom Numbers and Facilities	Prices (£) MIN	MAX
Regency House, 4 River Terrace, **Henley-on-Thames**, RG9 1BG ☎ (0491) 571133	♕♕♕	1⇔ 4⊞ 5⊡ ☜2 ♀ ⊞ SB ♙ ⊟ ⵑ	43.50 50.00	60.00 70.00
Peacock Hotel, **Henton**, Nr. Chinnor ☎ (0844) 53519	♕♕♕♕	6⇔ 6⊞ 12⊡ ☜ ♀ ⊞ ▣ ⊟ ⵑ	— —	45.00 55.00
Studley Priory Hotel, **Horton-cum-Studley**, OX9 1AZ ☎ (086735) 203 & 254	♕♕♕♕	6⇔ 13⊞ 19⊡ ☜ ♀ ⊞ ▣ SB ⚲ ♙ ⊟ ⊗ ⵑ	65.00 —	95.00 —
Manor Farm, **Kelmscott**, Nr. Lechlade, GL7 3HJ ☎ (0367) 52620	♕♕	2⊞ ☜ ▣ SB ⚲ ♙	— —	16.00 25.00
Bowood House Hotel, 238 Oxford Road, **Kidlington**, Oxford, OX5 1EB ☎ (0865) 842288		5⇔ 13⊞ 2⊞ 18⊡ ☜ ♀ ⊞ ▣ ⵑ	28.00 57.00	47.00 57.00
Cherwell Croft, 72 Church Street, **Kidlington**, OX5 2BB ☎ (08675) 3371	**L**	1⇔ 2⊞ ☜6 ▣ ♙	11.00 20.00	— —
Bould Farmhouse, Bould Farm, Bould, **Kingham**, OX7 6RT ☎ (060871) 8850	**L**	1⊞ 1⊞ ☜ ▣ ♙ ⊟	12.50 25.00	— 25.00
Conygree Gate Country House Hotel, Church Street, **Kingham**, OX7 6YA ☎ (060871) 389	♕♕	1⇔ 5⊞ 2⊞ 2⊡ ☜ ♀ ⊞ SB ⊟	20.00 32.00	— —
The Mill House Hotel and Restaurant, **Kingham**, OX7 6UH ☎ (060871) 8188	♕♕♕♕	20⊞ 1⊞ 21⊡ ☜5 ♀ ⊞ ▣ SB ⚲ ♙ ⊟ ⵑ	40.00 64.00	59.00 84.00
Fallowfields, Southmoor, **Kingston Bagpuize**, OX13 5BH ☎ (0865) 820416		3⊞ 1⊞ 4⊡ ☜10 ♀ ▣ ♙ ⊟ ⊗	24.00 48.00	— —
Hinds Head, Witney Road, **Kingston Bagpuize**, Nr. Abingdon, OX13 5AN ☎ (0865) 820204		1⇔ 2⊞ ♀ ⊞ ▣	15.00 22.00	— —
Old George Inn, **Leafield**, OX8 5NP ☎ (099387) 288	♕♕	2⊞ 2⊡ ☜ ♀ ⊞ ▣ SB ⵑ	14.00 28.00	18.00 32.00
Wynford House, 79 Main Road, **Long Hanborough**, Nr. Woodstock, OX7 2JX ☎ (0993) 881402	**L**	2⊞ 1⊞ 1⊡ ☜ ▣ SB	13.00 26.00	20.00 30.00
Manor Farm, **Lyford**, Wantage, OX12 0EG ☎ (023587) 204	♕♕	1⊞ 1⊞ ☜ ▣ SB ♙	14.50 26.00	16.00 30.00
Stable House, **Lyneham**, OX7 6QL ☎ (0993) 830000	**L**	1⊞ ▣ SB	— 45.00	— —

Establishment Name & Address	Crown Classification	Bedroom Numbers and Facilities	Prices (£) MIN	MAX
Jersey Arms Inn, **Middleton Stoney**, OX6 8SE ☎ (086989) 234	♛♛♛♛	16🛏 16⊞ 🛌 ♀ ⊞ 🅿 SB ▥ ♟	49.50 / 60.00	75.00 / 90.00
Belfry Hotel, **Milton Common**, Oxford, OX9 2JW ☎ (0844) 279381	♛♛♛♛	11🛏 48🛏 59⊞ 🛌 ♀ ⊞ 🅿 SB ▥ ✪ ♟	57.50 / 67.50	67.50 / 80.00
Hillborough Hotel, The Green, **Milton-under-Wychwood**, OX7 6JH ☎ (0993) 830501	♛♛♛	5🛏 1F 6⊞ 🛌 ♀ ⊞ 🅿 SB ✎	28.00 / 40.00	— / 42.00
Minster Lovell Mill Conference Centre, **Minster Lovell**, OX8 5RN ☎ (0993) 74441		21🛏 6🛏 27⊞ ♀ 🅿 ♠ ✪ ♟	— / —	— / —
The Old Swan, **Minster Lovell**, Nr. Witney, OX8 5RN ☎ (0993) 775614		2🛏 8🛏 10⊞ ♀ ⊞ 🅿 SB ✎ ♠ ▥ ♟	37.50 / 54.00	42.50 / 64.00
Forge Cottage, East End, **North Leigh**, Nr. Witney, OX8 6PZ ☎ (0993) 881120	♛♛	2🛏 1⊞ 🛌 🅿 ♠	— / 22.00	— / 28.00
Gorselands Bed & Breakfast, Boddington Lane, Nr. **North Leigh**, OX8 6PU ☎ (0993) 881202	Ⓛ	1🛏 1🛏 1F 1⊞ 🛌 🅿 ♠	20.00 / 30.00	20.00 / 30.00
The Athena Guest House, 253–255 Cowley Road, **Oxford**, OX4 1XQ ☎ (0865) 243124 & 243916	Ⓛ	3🛏 6🛏 3F 🛌5 🅿	13.00 / 25.00	15.00 / 29.00
Barclays Guest House, 1 Elsfield Way, Banbury Road, **Oxford** OX2 8EW ☎ (0865) 510327	♛♛	1🛏 3🛏 2F 3⊞ 🛌 🅿	15.00 / 30.00	18.00 / 36.00
Bravalla Guest House, 242 Iffley Road, **Oxford**, OX4 1SE ☎ (0865) 241326/250511	♛♛	3🛏 2F 4⊞ 🛌 ⊞ 🅿 SB	15.00 / 26.00	20.00 / 35.00
Bronte Guest House, 282 Iffley Road, **Oxford**, OX4 4AA ☎ (0865) 244594	♛♛	4🛏 1F 🛌 🅿 ✎	— / 22.00	— / 35.00
Brown's Guest House, 281 Iffley Road, **Oxford**, OX4 4AQ ☎ (0865) 246822	♛♛	2🛏 2🛏 2F 🛌 🅿	15.00 / 26.00	18.00 / 32.00
Casa Villa, 388 Banbury Road, **Oxford**, OX2 7PW ☎ (0865) 512642	Ⓛ	2🛏 3🛏 3F 6⊞ 🛌 ⊞ 🅿 SB ✎ ▥ ✪	20.00 / 35.00	22.00 / 37.00
Conifer Lodge, 159 Eynsham Road, Botley, **Oxford**, OX2 9NE ☎ (0865) 862280	♛♛	1🛏 1F 1⊞ 🛌 🅿	12.00 / 22.00	16.00 / 38.00

Establishment Name & Address	Crown Classification	Bedroom Numbers and Facilities	Prices (£) MIN	MAX
Cotswold Lodge Hotel, 66A Banbury Road, **Oxford**, OX2 6JP ☎ (0865) 512121/9	♔♔♔♔	20🛏 30♔ 2🅕 52⊞ ⛬ ♿ ♨ 🅿 SB 🏤 🎪 🍴	🛏 62.50 ♨ 77.50	67.50 85.50
Eastgate Hotel, The High, **Oxford**, OX1 4BE ☎ (0865) 248244		13🛏 29♔ 1🅕 43⊞ ⛬ ♿ ♨ 🅿 SB 🔌 🏤 🍴	🛏 69.00 ♨ 81.00	77.00 00.00
Mrs. C. Evans, 438 Marston Road, Marston, **Oxford**, OX3 0JE ☎ (0865) 721023	Ⓛ	1🛏 1♔ ⛬ 🅿 🏤	🛏 10.00 ♨ 20.00	11.00 22.00
Greenviews, 95 Sunningwell Road, **Oxford**, OX1 4SY ☎ (0865) 249603	♔♔	4🛏 3♔ 1⊞ ♿ ⛬ 🅿 ❂	🛏 — ♨ —	14.00 33.00
Highfield West, 188 Cumnor Hill, **Oxford**, OX2 9PJ ☎ (0865) 863007	♔♔♔	2🛏 2♔ 1🅕 3⊞ ⛬ 🅿 SB 🏤 ❂	🛏 17.00 ♨ 35.00	17.00 37.00
The Lawns, 12 Manor Road, South Hinksey, **Oxford**, OX1 5AS ☎ (0865) 739980	♔♔	2♔ 1⊞ ⛬ 🅿	🛏 — ♨ 27.00	— 30.00
Linton Lodge Hotel, 9–13 Linton Road, **Oxford**, OX2 6UJ ☎ (0865) 53461	♔♔♔♔	16🛏 54♔ 1🅕 71⊞ ♿ ⛬ ♨ 🅕 🅿 SB 🔌 🏤 🍴	🛏 70.00 ♨ 85.00	95.00 115.00
The Old Black Horse Hotel, 102 St. Clements, **Oxford**, OX4 1AR ☎ (0865) 244691		1🛏 5♔ 2🅕 8⊞ ⛬ ♨ 🅿 🏤	🛏 38.00 ♨ 58.00	48.00 70.00
The Old Parsonage Hotel, Ltd. 1–3 Banbury Road, **Oxford**, OX2 6NN ☎ (0865) 310210	♔♔	7🛏 26♔ 2🅕 1⊞ ⛬ ♨ 🅕 🅿 🏤 🏰	🛏 27.00 ♨ 40.00	38.00 48.00
Oxford Moat House, Wolvercote Roundabout, **Oxford**, OX2 8AL ☎ (0865) 59933		143♔ 12🅕 155⊞ ⛬ ♨ 🅕 🅿 SB ❂ 🍴	🛏 75.00 ♨ 90.00	75.00 —
Pickwicks Guest House, 17 London Road, Headington, **Oxford**, OX3 7SP ☎ (0865) 750487/69413	♔♔♔♔	2🛏 8♔ 2🅕 10⊞ ⛬ 🅿 🍴	🛏 18.00 ♨ 30.00	28.00 40.00
Pine Castle Hotel, 290 Iffley Road, **Oxford**, OX4 1AE ☎ (0865) 241497/727230	♔♔	1🛏 2♔ 2🅕 ⛬ 🅿	🛏 16.00 ♨ 31.00	17.00 34.00
The Randolph, Beaumont Street, **Oxford** OX1 2LN ☎ (0865) 247481		42🛏 62♔ 5🅕 109⊞ ⛬ ♨ 🅕 SB 🔌 🏤 🍴	🛏 75.00 ♨ 96.00	86.00 105.00
River Hotel, 17 Botley Road, **Oxford**, OX2 0AA ☎ (0865) 243475	♔♔♔	14🛏 7♔ 3🅕 17⊞ ⛬ ♨ 🅕 🅿 🏤 🍴	🛏 30.00 ♨ 40.00	42.50 52.00

Establishment Name & Address	Crown Classification	Bedroom Numbers and Facilities	Prices (£) MIN	MAX
Royal Oxford Hotel, Park End Street, **Oxford**, OX1 1HR ☎ (0865) 248432	♛♛♛	12⇥ 11🛏 2🅵 12⊞ ⟟ ⚲ ⌧ 🅿 SB 🚗 ⚑	32.00 43.00	54.00 70.00
Ryan's Guest House, 164 Banbury Road, Summertown, **Oxford**, OX2 7BU ☎ (0865) 58876	🄻	3🛏 1🅵 ⟟ 🅿 🚗 ⌖	13.00 26.00	17.00 34.00
Shannon Guest House, 329 Cowley Road, **Oxford**, OX4 2AQ ☎ (0865) 247558	🄻	3🛏 ⟟5 🅿	— 27.00	— 31.00
Sportsview Guest House, 108 Abingdon Road, **Oxford**, OX1 4PX ☎ (0865) 244268	♛♛	5⇥ 7🛏 4🅵 2⊞ ⟟ ⌧ 🅿 🏮	13.00 24.00	15.00 35.00
The Tree Hotel, Church Way, Iffley, **Oxford**, OX4 4EY ☎ (0865) 775974 & 778190	♛♛	3⇥ 3🛏 1🅵 2⊞ ⟟ ⚲ ⌧ 🅿 SB 🚗 ⚑	45.00 65.00	47.50 75.00
Victoria Hotel, 180 Abingdon Road, **Oxford**, OX1 4RA ☎ (0865) 724536		7⇥ 14🛏 2🅵 14⊞ ⟟ ⚲ ⌧ 🅿 SB 🚗 ⚑	35.50 47.50	45.50 55.50
Welcome Lodge, Peartree Roundabout, Woodstock Road, **Oxford**, OX2 8JZ ☎ (0865) 54301		59🛏 41🅵 100⊞ ♿ ⟟ ⚲ ⌧ 🅿 SB 🚗 ⚑	50.00 —	— —
The Welsh Pony Hotel, 48 George Street, **Oxford**, OX1 2AQ ☎ (0865) 242998/725087	🄻	3⇥ 5🛏 2🅵 ⟟ ⚲	15.00 26.00	— —
The Westminster Guest House, 350 Iffley Road, **Oxford**, OX4 4AU ☎ (0865) 250924	♛	1⇥ 2🛏 🅿	15.00 26.00	18.00 28.00
Westwood Country Hotel, Hinksey Hill, **Oxford**, OX1 5BG ☎ (0865) 735408	♛♛♛♛	11⇥ 13🛏 2🅵 27⊞ ⟟ ⚲ ⌧ 🅿 SB 🚗 ⚑	35.00 55.00	45.00 82.00
The White House, 315 Iffley Road, **Oxford**, OX4 4AG ☎ (0865) 244524	🄻	6🛏 2🅵 ⟟ 🅿 SB ⌖	17.00 30.00	17.00 30.00
Willow Reaches Private Hotel, 1 Wytham Street, **Oxford**, OX1 4SU ☎ (0865) 721545/243767	♛♛♛	3⇥ 4🛏 2🅵 5⊞ ⟟ ⚲ ⌧ 🅿 SB 🚗	19.00 32.00	22.00 39.00
The Shaven Crown Hotel, High Street, **Shipton-under-Wychwood**, OX7 6BA ☎ (0993) 830330	♛♛♛	1⇥ 7🛏 1🅵 8⊞ ⟟ ⚲ ⌧ 🅿 SB ⌖ 🏮 🚗 ⚑	24.00 56.00	24.00 56.00
Kings Arms Hotel, **Skirmett**, Henley-on-Thames, RG9 6TG ☎ (049163) 247	🄻	3🛏 1🅵 2⊞ ⟟ ⚲ ⌧ 🅿 SB 🏮	— 42.00	— 49.00

Establishment Name & Address	Crown Classification	Bedroom Numbers and Facilities	Prices (£) MIN	MAX
Jersey Manor Farmhouse, **Somerton**, Oxford, OX5 4NO ☎ (0869) 345414		2🛏 2🄵 ⌖8 ♀ 🛁 ⊙ 🍴	15.00 28.00	15.00 28.00
The Old Rectory, Church End, **Standlake**, Nr. Witney, OX8 7SG ☎ (0865) 300559	👑👑👑	4🛏 4⊡ ⌖5 🅿 SB 🌿 🛁	20.00 30.00	32.00 55.00
Hopcrofts Holt Hotel, Banbury Road, **Steeple Aston**, Oxford, OX5 3QQ ☎ (0869) 40259	👑👑👑👑	4🛏 57🛏 2🄵 63⊡ ⌖ ♀ ⊞ 🅿 🛁 ⊙ 🍴	48.00 60.00	— —
Steventon House Hotel, Milton Hill, **Steventon**, Nr. Abingdon, OX13 6AB ☎ (0235) 831223	👑👑👑👑	10🛏 13🛏 2🄵 25⊡ ♿ ⌖ ♀ ⊞ 🅿 🍴	44.00 55.00	— —
Timsbury Hotel, 26 High Street, **Steventon**, OX13 6RS ☎ (0235) 831254/831685		4🛏 5🛏 9⊡ ⌖ ♀ ⊞ 🅿 SB 🍴	40.00 48.00	— —
The Spread Eagle Hotel, Cornmarket, **Thame**, OX9 2BW ☎ (084421) 3661	👑👑👑👑	5🛏 16🛏 1🄵 22⊡ ⌖ ♀ ⊞ 🅿 SB 🌿 🛁 🍴	62.00 73.00	70.00 80.00
Thatchers Hotel & Restaurant, 29–30 Lower High Street, **Thame**, OX9 2AA ☎ (084421) 2146/3058		4🛏 6🛏 10⊡ ♿ ⌖ ♀ ⊞ 🅿 🛁 🍴	46.50 57.50	48.50 75.00
Tubney Warren House Hotel, Faringdon Road, **Tubney**, Abingdon, OX13 5QJ ☎ (0865) 390400		1🛏 4🛏 1🄵 6⊡ ⌖8 ⊞ 🅿 SB 🛁 🍴	53.00 —	61.00 —
The George Hotel, High Street, **Wallingford**, OX10 0BS ☎ (0491) 36665	👑👑👑👑	14🛏 24🛏 1🄵 39⊡ ⌖ ♀ ⊞ 🅿 SB 🌿 🛁 🍴	49.50 —	53.50 67.50
The Shillingford Bridge Hotel, Shillingford, **Wallingford**, OX10 8LZ ☎ (086732) 8567	👑👑👑👑	14🛏 22🛏 1🄵 37⊡ ♿ ⌖ ♀ ⊞ 🅿 🛁 🍴 ⊙ 🍴	50.00 65.00	60.00 90.00
The Springs Hotel, North Stoke, **Wallingford**, OX9 6BE ☎ (0491) 36687		3🛏 25🛏 5🄵 33⊡ ♿ ⌖ ♀ ⊞ 🅿 SB 🌿 🛁 🍴 ⊙ 🍴	65.00 105.00	95.00 130.00
The Bear Hotel, Market Place, **Wantage**, OX12 8AB ☎ (02357) 66366		5🛏 29🛏 34⊡ ⌖ ♀ ⊞ SB 🌿 🛁 🍴	29.50 42.00	47.50 70.50
The Well House Restaurant and Hotel, 34–40 High Street, **Watlington**, OX9 5PY ☎ (0491761) 3333	👑👑👑👑	1🛏 8🛏 9⊡ ⌖ ♀ ⊞ 🅿 SB 🌿 🛁 🍴	32.00 54.00	44.50 64.00
Weston Manor Hotel, **Weston-on-the-Green**, Bicester, OX6 8QL ☎ (0869) 50621	👑👑👑👑	37🛏 2🄵 39⊡ ♿ ⌖ ♀ ⊞ 🅿 SB 🌿 🛁 🍴 ⊙ 🍴	75.00 98.00	82.50 105.00

Establishment Name & Address	Crown Classification	Bedroom Numbers and Facilities	Prices (£) MIN MAX	
Ambury Close Farm, Barnard Gate, Nr. **Witney**, OX8 6XE ☎ (0865) 881356	🅛	3🛏 2🇫 ⛵1 ♀🅿	18.00 30.00	20.00 32.00
Bird in Hand, Whiteoak Green, Hailey, Nr. **Witney**, OX8 5XP ☎ (0993) 86321		4🛏 10🛏 2🇫 16⊞ ♿ ⛵♀🖾🅿 SB ✎ ♟	29.50 42.50	36.50 49.50
The Court Inn, 43 Bridge Street, **Witney**, OX8 6DA ☎ (0993) 703228	♔♔	1🛏 4🛏 2🇫 2⊞ ⛵♀🅿 SB ✎ 🏠 ♟	15.00 25.00	21.00 30.00
The Marlborough Hotel, 28 Market Square, **Witney**, OX8 7BB ☎ (0993) 776353		7🛏 14🛏 21⊞ ⛵♀🖾🅿 SB 🏠🚗 ♟	34.50 46.00	38.00 55.00
The Rose Revived Inn, Newbridge, Nr. **Witney**, OX8 7QD ☎ (0865) 300221		1🛏 6🛏 3⊞ ⛵♀🖾🅿 ✎🏠🚗	30.00 40.00	— —
The Witney Lodge Hotel, Ducklington Lane, **Witney**, OX8 7TJ ☎ (0993) 779777		63🛏 7🇫 70⊞ ♿⛵♀🖾🅿 SB ♟	24.00 44.00	59.00 72.00
Bear Hotel and Restaurant, Park Street, **Woodstock**, OX7 1SZ ☎ (0993) 811511		5🛏 39🛏 1🇫 45⊞ ⛵♀🖾🅿 SB ✎🏠🚗♟	69.00 99.00	75.00 150.00
Feathers Hotel, Market Street, **Woodstock**, OX7 1SX ☎ (0993) 812291	♔♔♔♔	1🛏 14🛏 15⊞ ⛵♀🖾🅿 SB ✎🏠♟	60.00 75.00	78.00 108.00
Kings Arms Hotel, Market Square, **Woodstock**, OX7 1ST ☎ (0993) 812073/811592		3🛏 7🛏 10⊞ ⛵♀🖾 SB ✎🏠♟	50.00 66.00	59.00 77.00
Marlborough Arms Hotel, Oxford Street, **Woodstock**, OX7 1TS ☎ (0993) 811227		2🛏 9🛏 2🇫 10⊞ ⛵♀🖾🅿 SB 🏠🚗♟	40.00 60.00	50.00 65.00
The Star Inn, Market Square, **Woodstock** ☎ (0993) 811373		4🛏 4⊞ ⛵♀🖾	30.00 40.00	35.00 49.00
Mrs. Burge, 1 Vermont Drive, Old Woodstock, **Woodstock** ☎ (0993) 811344		1🛏 2🛏 1⊞ 🅿	— 12.00	— 14.00

Establishment Name & Address	Crown Classification	Bedroom Numbers and Facilities	Prices (£) MIN MAX	

Adjacent Counties

Establishment Name & Address	Crown Classification	Bedroom Numbers and Facilities	MIN	MAX
Aarons of Barnet, 56 Bedford Avenue, **High Barnet** EN5 2ER ☎ 01-441 4901		7🛏 3🅕 4⊞ ⅃ 🕭 🅿 SB ✪	20.00 30.00	30.00 40.00
Blunsdon House Hotel, **Blunsdon**, Swindon, Wiltshire. SN2 4AD ☎ (0793) 721701	♛♛♛♛♛	2🛏 71🛏 16🅕 89⊞ ♿ ⅃ 🍷 🕭 🅿 SB ✎ ✪ ⚒	75.00 82.50	85.00 92.50
The Cotswold House Hotel & Restaurant, **Chipping Camden**, Gloucestershire, GL55 6AN ☎ (0386) 840330	♛♛♛♛	3🛏 12🛏 15⊞ ⅃8 🍷 🕭 🅿 SB 🏧 📠 ⚒	44.00 75.00	54.00 99.00
Fleece Hotel, Market Place, **Cirencester**, Gloucestershire, GL7 4NZ ☎ (0285) 658507	♛♛♛♛	2🛏 13🛏 4🅕 19⊞ ⅃ 🍷 🕭 🅿 SB ✎ 🏧 📠 ⚒	58.95	68.95 —
Whatley Manor Hotel, **Easton Grey**, Malmesbury, Wiltshire, SN16 0RB ☎ (0666) 822888	♛♛♛♛	22🛏 3🅕 25⊞ ⅃ 🍷 🕭 🅿 SB ✎ 🏧 📠 ⚒	66.00 73.00	92.00 106.00
The Mansion House at Grim's Dyke, Old Redding, **Harrow Weald**, Middlesex, HA3 6SH ☎ 01–954 4227	♛♛♛♛	2🛏 45🛏 47⊞ ⅃ 🍷 🕭 🅿 SB ✎ 🏧 📠 ⚒	69.50	94.50 —
Lower Slaughter Manor, **Lower Slaughter**, Gloucestershire, GL54 2HP ☎ (0451) 20456	♛♛♛	2🛏 17🛏 19⊞ ⅃8 🍷 🕭 🅿 SB ✎ 🏧 📠 ✪ ⚒	75.00 95.00	— —
Stanwell Hall Hotel, Stanwell, **Staines**, Surrey, TW19 7PW ☎ (07842) 52292	♛♛♛	11🛏 9🛏 1🅕 16⊞ ⅃ 🍷 🕭 🅿 SB ⚒	34.50 50.00	63.00 73.50
Snooty Fox Hotel, Market Place, **Tetbury**, Gloucestershire, GL8 8DD ☎ (0666) 502436	♛♛♛	1🛏 11🛏 12⊞ ⅃ 🍷 🕭 SB 🏧 📠 ⚒	62.00 68.00	78.00 84.00
Lords of The Manor Hotel, **Upper Slaughter**, Nr. Cheltenham, Gloucestershire ☎ (0451) 20243	♛♛♛♛	2🛏 28🛏 30⊞ ♿ ⅃ 🍷 🕭 🅿 SB ✎ 🏧 📠 ✪ ⚒	— 85.00	65.00 125.00

SELF-CATERING HOLIDAY HOMES

Establishment	Approved	No. of Units (No. of persons per unit)	Facilities	Price range per unit per week
The Boathouse Flat, High Street, **Goring-on-Thames**, Reading, Berkshire RG8 9AB ☎ (0491) 872394	Ⓐ	1 (4)	⛱ 🅿 ⊘ ▦ ⊡ ▭ ⊞ 1–12	£200–£245
Yaffles, Red Shute Hill, **Hermitage**, Nr. Newbury, Berkshire RG16 9QH ☎ (0635) 201100	Ⓐ	1 (4)	⛱ 🅿 ◉ ▦ ⊡ ▭ ⊞ 1–12	£120 – £180
Mapledurham Estate, Mapledurham House, **Mapledurham**, Reading, Berkshire RG4 7TR ☎ (0734) 723350	Ⓐ	10 (2 –7)	⛱ 🅿 ◉ ▦ Ⓜ ⊡ ▭ ⊞ ⊩ 1–12	£85 – £300
Wallace Farm Cottage, Wallace Farm, **Dinton**, Nr. Aylesbury, Buckinghamshire HP17 8UR ☎ (0296) 748660	Ⓐ	2 (3 –6)	♿ ⛱ 🅿 ◉ ▦ ⊡ ▭ ⊞ ⊩ 1–12	£110 – £200
The Wheatsheaf, **Weedon**, Nr. Aylesbury, Buckinghamshire HP22 4NS ☎ (0296) 641581	Ⓐ	3 (3 –5)	⛱ 🅿 ◉ ▦ ⊡ ⊞ ⊩ 1–12	£100 – £155
Lee Valley Park, Broxbourne Meadows, Mill Lane, **Broxbourne**, Hertfordshire EN10 6QS ☎ (0992) 446677		4 (5 –6)	♿ ⛱ 🅿 ◉ ⊡ 3–10	£59 – £113
Campus Holidays, Bishops Rise, **Hatfield**, Hertfordshire AL10 9JL ☎ (07072) 79064	Ⓐ	30 (3 –6)	♿ ⛱ 🅿 ◉ ▦ ⊡ ▭ ⊞ 7–9	£135 – £215
The Mill, Witney Street, **Burford**, Oxfordshire OX8 4DN ☎ (099382) 2379	Ⓐ	5 (2 –5)	⛱ 🅿 ◉ ▦ ⊡ ▭ ⊞ ⊩ 1–12	£120 – £330
Widford Farm Cottages, Widford Manor, **Burford**, Oxfordshire OX8 4DU ☎ (099382) 2152	Ⓐ	7 (3 –8)	⛱ 🅿 ◉ ⊡ ▭ ⊞ ⊩ 1–12	£90 – £245

Establishment	Approved	No. of Units (No. of persons per unit)	Facilities	Price range per unit per week
Views Farm Barns, Views Farm, **Great Milton**, Oxfordshire OX9 7NW ☎ (0844) 279352	Ⓐ	6 (2 –4)	♿ ⛵ 🅿 ◎ 🚬 🗓 ⊐ 🖵 ⋔ 1–12	£102 – £228
Foxholes, **Hook Norton**, c/o Faraday House, Sibford Ferris, Banbury, Oxfordshire OX15 5RF ☎ (0295) 78339		1 (4–5)	⛵6 🅿 ◎ ⌀ 🗓 ⊐ 🖵 1–12	£175 – £245
Millstone Cottage, Bells Lane, **Hook Norton**, Nr. Banbury, Oxfordshire OX15 5RU ☎ (029578) 371	Ⓐ	1 (5)	⛵ 🅿 ◎ 🚬 🗓 ⊐ 🖵 1–12	£100 – £200
Honeystone Cottage, 1 Cozens Lane, **Kingham**, Oxfordshire OX7 6YZ c/o Summer Cottages Ltd. ☎ (0305) 251130	Ⓐ	1 (4)	⛵ 🅿 ◎ 🚬 🗓 ⊐ 1–12	£133 – £233
Milton Manor Flat, Milton Manor, **Milton**, Nr. Abingdon, Oxfordshire OX14 4EN ☎ (0235) 831287	Ⓐ	1 (4)	⛵ ◎ 🗓 ⊐ 🖵 1–12	£105 – £160
Morrell Hall, John Garne Way, Marston, **Oxford**, OX3 0TU ☎ (0865) 819111 (0865) 819100	Ⓐ	14 (6)	♿ ⛵ 🅿 ◎ 🚬 🗓 ⊐ 🖵 ⋔ 4, 7–9	£255 – £315
Butts Slade Bungalow & Cara-Mia Cottage, **Sibford Gower**, Oxfordshire OX15 5RU ☎ (029578) 371	Ⓐ	2 (4 –5)	⛵ 🅿 ◎ 🗓 ⊐ 🖵 ⋔ 1–12	£85 – £145
Dairy, Stable & Garden Cottages, Mongewell Park Farm, Mongewell, **Wallingford**, Oxfordshire OX10 8BS ☎ (0491) 37284	Ⓐ	3 (4)	♿ ⛵ 🅿 ◎ 🚬 Ⓜ ⊐ 🖵 1–12	£100 – £170
Gleann Cottages, Woodstock Road, **Witney**, Oxfordshire OX8 6UH ☎ (0993) 774185	Ⓐ	8 (2 –4)	⛵ 🅿 ◎ 🚬 Ⓜ 🗓 ⊐ 🖵 ⋔ 1–12	£115 – £178

CAMPING & CARAVAN PARKS

Establishment	Quality Grading	Total No. of pitches	Facilities	Min. price per pitch per night
Hurley Caravan & Camping Park, Shepherds Lane, **Hurley**, Berkshire SL6 5NE ☎ (062882) 3501 (Office)	✓✓✓	350	⊞ ☒ 🜲 ☯ ⅄ 🜚 ↑ 3–10	£6.00
Dobbs Weir Caravan Park, Essex Road, **Hoddesdon**, Hertfordshire EN11 0AS ☎ (0992) 462090	✓✓✓✓	100	⊞ ☒ 🜲 ☯ ⅄ 🖫 ↑ 4–10	£5.50
Benson Cruisers Camping & Caravan Park, **Benson**, Oxfordshire OX9 8SJ ☎ (0491) 38304	✓✓✓✓	30	⊞ ☒ ♀ 🜲 ☯ ⅄ ⅃ 🖫 ↑ 4–10	£5.00
Cassington Mill Caravan Park, Eynsham Road, **Cassington**, Oxfordshire OX8 1DB ☎ (0865) 881081	✓✓✓	83	⊞ ☒ 🜲 ☯ ⅄ ↑ 4–10	£4.50
Cotswold View Caravan and Camping Site, Enstone Road, **Charlbury**, Oxfordshire OX7 3JH ☎ (0608) 810314	✓✓✓✓✓	90	⊞ ☒ 🜲 ☯ ⅄ ⅃ 🖫 ↑ 4–10	£5.00
Swiss Farm International Camping, Swiss Farm, Marlow Road, **Henley-on-Thames**, Oxfordshire RG9 2HY ☎ (0491) 573419		180	⊞ ☒ ♀ 🜲 ☯ ⅄ ⅃ 🖫 ↑ 3–10	£4.00
Oxford Camping International, 426 Abingdon Road, **Oxford**, OX1 4XN ☎ (0865) 246551	✓✓✓✓	129	⊞ ☒ ♀ 🜲 ☯ ⅄ ⅃ 🖫 ↑ 1–12	£5.80
Hardwick Parks Ltd., Downs Road, **Standlake**, Oxfordshire OX8 7TV ☎ (086731) 501		150	⊞ ☒ 🜲 ☯ ⅄ ⅃ 🖫 ↑ 4–10	£5.00
Lincoln Farm Park, High Street, **Standlake**, Oxfordshire OX8 7RH ☎ (086731) 239	✓✓✓✓✓	70	⊞ ☒ 🜲 ☯ ⅄ ⅃ 🖫 ↑ 4–10	£5.50

116

YOUTH HOSTELS

Bradenham Y.H.A.
The Village Hall, Bradenham,
High Wycombe, Bucks
Tel: (08956) 73188

Jordans Y.H.A.
Welders Lane, Jordans,
Beaconsfield, Bucks HP9 2SN
Tel: (02407) 3135

Oxford Y.H.A.
Jack Straw's Lane, Oxford
OX3 0DW
Tel: (0865) 62997

St Albans Y.H.A.
Fairshot Court, Woodcock
Hill, Sandridge, St Albans,
Herts AL4 9ED
Tel: (0727) 51854

Windsor Y.H.A.
Edgeworth House, Mill Lane,
Windsor, Berks SL4 5JE
Tel: (0753) 861710

Charlbury Y.H.A.
The Laurels, The Slade,
Charlbury, Oxon OX7 3SJ
Tel: (0608) 810202

Ivinghoe Y.H.A.
The Old Brewery House,
Ivinghoe, Leighton Buzzard,
Beds LU7 9EP
Tel: (0296) 668251

Milton Keynes Y.H.A.
Manor Farm, Vicarage Road,
Bradwell, Milton Keynes,
Bucks MK13 9AJ
Tel: (0908) 310944

Ridgeway Y.H.A.
The Court Hill Ridgeway
Centre, Court Hill, Wantage,
Oxon.
Tel: (02357) 60253

Streatley Y.H.A.
Hill House, Reading Road,
Streatley, Berks RG8 9JJ
Tel: (0491) 872278

Eating and Drinking

The following establishments, all members of the Thames and Chilterns Tourist Board, represent a range of pubs and restaurants in the region. They offer a selection of high-quality, good-value food and drink.

Berkshire

Ascot Guinea, Mill Ride Estate, Mill Ride, **North Ascot**
Tel: (0344) 886737
An elegant and traditional restaurant serving the finest British food including venison from the Crown Estate.

Butchers Arms, Blounts Court, **Sonning Common** nr Reading
Tel: (0734) 723101
A traditional country village inn serving a tasty range of home-cooked food.

Country Kitchen Restaurant, 3 King Edward Court, **Windsor**
Tel: (0753) 868681.
A modern restaurant with carvery and self-service in Windsor's shopping centre.

The Grouse and Claret, Stoke Row Road, **Kingwood Common**, Nr Henley on Thames
Tel: (04917) 359
Comfortable and spacious bar, with well-appointed restaurant, set in beautiful Chiltern countryside.

House on the Bridge, Windsor Bridge, **Eton**
Tel: (0753) 860914
A smart restaurant on the bank of the Thames opposite Windsor Castle.

New Mill Restaurant, **Eversley**, Nr Reading
Tel: (0734) 732277
A charming 16th-C. mill on the River Blackwater, with the working mill wheel and mill stream running through the middle.

Ostrich Inn, High Street, **Colnbrook**, nr. Slough
Tel: (0753) 682628
One of the four oldest inns in England, founded in 1106, with a history of murder.

Two Roses Restaurant, High Street, **Cookham**
Tel: (06285) 20875
Friendly family-run restaurant in a 400-year-old cottage; morning coffee, lunch and dinner by candlelight.

Warrener Restaurant, Warren Row, nr **Wargrave**
Tel: (0628) 822803
A country cottage restaurant with a pretty dining room, serving a menu of French and Swedish dishes.

Yew Tree Inn, **Highclere**, Newbury
Tel: (0635) 253360
A traditional English inn, dating from the 17th-C., with priest-hole, original brickwork and log fires.

Buckinghamshire

Rectory Farm Restaurant, Buckingham Road, **Hardwick**, nr Aylesbury
Tel: (0296) 641204
A popular restaurant, a charming conversion of farm buildings.

Royal Standard of England, Forty Green, **Beaconsfield**
Tel: (0494) 673382
A world-famous, 900-year-old free house, with wood panelling and beams, good food, beer and wine.

Hertfordshire

The Barns, Knebworth Park, **Stevenage**
Tel: (0438) 813825
Two 400-year-old tithe barns beside Knebworth House, with self-service restaurant in summer and banqueting all year round.

Old Swan Tea Shop, Hare Street, **Buntingford**
Tel: (076389) 265
A beautifully restored 15th-C. building in this pretty village.

Plough Inn, **Great Munden**, Nr Ware
Tel: (092084) 335
A country pub with regular entertainment on the famous 'Compton' Cinema Organ with guest organists.

Oxfordshire

The Ark, Wantage Road, **Marcham**, nr Abingdon
Tel: (0865) 391470
A 16th-C. coaching inn with two restaurants: the Ock Room serving inexpensive meals and the Corinthian Room for à la carte.

Crumpled Horn, Heathfield Village, **Bletchingdon**
Tel: (0869) 50913
A licensed restaurant and large function room in a leisure village with golf driving range and equestrian centre.

Kingswell Farm Restaurant and Hotel, Reading Road, **Harwell**, Nr Didcot
Tel: (0235) 833043
A traditional English restaurant in a converted farmhouse, with polished wood beams and floors.

Moonlight Tandoori Restaurant, 58 Cowley Road, **Oxford**
Tel: (0865) 240275
An exciting menu of classic Indian and Tandoori cooking in a stylish restaurant with hand-painted murals.

The Plough at **Kelmscott**, Kelmscott, nr Lechlade
Tel: (0367) 52358
A country pub and restaurant with stone-flagged floor in the hamlet where William Morris lived.

The White Hart, St Andrews Road, **Old Headington**, Oxford
Tel: (0865) 61737
A quaint little pub serving good-value bar meals in the pretty village of Old Headington on the outskirts of the city.

White Hart Inn and Restaurant, **Fyfield**
Tel: (0865) 390585
An ancient inn and restaurant with minstrels' gallery, with an innovative bar menu.

The Red Lion, Nottingham Fee, **Blewbury**, nr Didcot
Tel: (0235) 850403
An old, beamed pub, no machines, no music, with garden, restaurant and log fires.

The Seven Stars, **Marsh Baldon** nr Nuneham Courtenay, Oxford
Tel: (086738) 255
A pretty white washed pub on the edge of the village green, with home-cooked bar meals.

The Windmill, Windrush Valley Park, **Asthall**, nr Burford
Tel: (099382) 2594
A traditional Cotswold stone restaurant offering classic English fare in a rural setting.

Conference Venues

Name and Address	Capacity Residential	Non-Residential	Description
Beauchamp Centre, Barford Road, **Bloxham**, Nr Banbury, Oxon OX15 4EZ Tel: (0295) 720988	N/A	100	Modern squash club with function meeting room and reception area restaurant.
Brunel University, Conference Office, **Uxbridge**, Middx UB8 3PH Tel: (0895) 74000 Ext 2440 Telex: 261173	600	—	Campus facilities with lecture theatre and seminar rooms, close to Heathrow.
Buttermilk Stud Management Centre, Barford St Michael, **Nr Banbury**, Oxon. Tel: (0295) 721935	11	40	Secluded Oxfordshire farmhouse with facilities for exclusive meetings and comfortable accommodation.
Castle Ashby House, **Castle Ashby**, Nr Northampton, Northants NN7 1LQ Tel: (0601) 29234 Telex: 83343 CAH	15	380	16th-century ancestral home of the Marquess of Northampton available for business and hospitality events.
Chartridge Centre, Chartridge, **Chesham**, Bucks HP5 2TU Tel: (024020) 484	44	80	Self-contained conference centre in beautiful grounds with pub and leisure facilities. Close to London & M25.
Cranfield Conference Centre, Wharley End, **Cranfield**, Bedford MK43 0HG Tel: (0234) 751077	112	130	Five miles from the M1, Cranfield combines hotel and conference facilities with the technology of Cranfield Institute.
Christ Church, **Oxford** OX1 1DP Tel: (0865) 276174	300	300	One of the largest and most historic of the Oxford colleges, founded by Henry VIII.
Formula Williams Building, Williams Grand Prix Engineering, Basil Hill Road, **Didcot**, Oxon OX11 7HW Tel: (0235) 815161	—	60	Purpose-built conference centre with a display of Williams Formula-One Cars.
The Leander Club, **Henley on Thames**, Oxon RG9 2LP Tel: (0491) 575782	12	80	A prestigious private rowing club on the bank of the River Thames overlooking the Regatta course. Large function/meeting/private dining facilities.
Hatfield Polytechnic, **Hatfield**, Herts AL10 9AB Tel: (07272) 79061	1000	450	Year-round facilities for activities from meetings and social occasions to fairs and conferences at its three major sites at Hatfield, Hertford and Radlett.
The Manor House, **Little Milton**, Oxon OX9 7QB Tel: (08446) 368	—	—	Country manor house catering for exclusive meetings and functions.
Minster Lovell Mill Conference Centre, **Minster Lovell**, Oxon OX8 5RN Tel: (0993) 774441	33	50	A high-quality conference centre for small groups in a beautiful riverside country setting with excellent service and cuisine.
Rossway, **Berkhamsted**, Herts HP4 3TZ Tel: (0442) 865160/875634	—	40	An accessible prestigious country house venue for meetings or hospitality. Clay shooting, archery and exciting activities are available. Marquees for large events including weddings, product launches or fashion shows.
Royal Agricultural College, **Cirencester**, Gloucester GL7 6JS Tel: (0285) 2531	338	832	In the heart of the Cotswolds, the college is in a 30-acre site and combines modern facilities with Victorian elegance.
Worcester College, **Oxford** OX1 2HB Tel: (0865) 278335	150	140	Available Jan, Mar–Apr, Jul–Sept only. An historic college with modern facilities.

WINDSOR

Sir Christopher Wren's House Hotel

* Beautiful Orangerie restaurant overlooking the Thames and Eton Bridge. Fixed price à la carte luncheon. Extensive à la carte dinner menu.
* Theatre Weekend breaks in conjunction with the Theatre Royal, Windsor.
* 39 bedrooms, many with views of the river and castle, en suite, colour t.v., tea/coffee making facilities, four-poster beds.
* Magnificent wedding reception/banqueting facilities.
* Conferences – 5 suites.
* 60-seater Terrace Restaurant serving lunches, afternoon tea and dinner in summer.

Thames Street, Windsor, Berks SL4 1PX. Telephone No. 0753–861354
Fax 0753–860172   Telex 847938 WRENH SG

READING

THE GREAT HOUSE AT SONNING

* Delightful Moorings Restaurant. Fixed price Table D'Hote luncheon, extensive evening à la carte menu.
  * Hideaway Bistro, carvery luncheons, evening à la carte, log fires, original beams, cosy atmosphere.
* Riverside Weekend breaks.
* Wedding Receptions a specialty.
* Conference and banqueting facilities – 7 suites.
* 37 en suite bedrooms, colour t.v., tea and coffee making facilities, trouser press, seven four poster beds.

Thames Street, Sonning on Thames, Berks RG4 0UT. Telephone No.
0734–692277, Telex 849031 GREAT G, Fax 0734–441296.
Greenstar Hotels plc

Turn back the pages of history this summer at one of the many impressive English Heritage properties in this area.

Lovers of fine gardens should make straight for Wrest Park, where they will see the whole history of English gardening, from 1700 to 1850, unfold before them in acres of stunning splendour. Intersecting alleys provide delightful vistas of the many garden buildings and ornaments. The house itself was inspired by 18th century French models, and the state rooms are open to the public. Wrest Park House and Gardens is less than a mile east of Silsoe, just off the A6, north of Luton.

Fire destroyed the great house to which Rycote Chapel was once attached, but the beautiful 15th century Chapel itself survived. It can be found today three miles south west of Thame off the M40 and features a pew built specially for Charles I.

Tradition has it that the skeleton of Lord Lovell was discovered during repair work to Minster Lovell Hall, centuries after he had mysteriously disappeared. Today's visitor can explore the dramatic ruins of this beautiful 15th century manor house in its lovely riverside setting, three miles west of Witney.

Other sites of historical interest in the area include North Leigh Roman Villa, with its intricate mosaic tiled floor, and the wall paintings and stained glass at Bushmead Priory.

History comes alive with English Heritage, and the key to the past can be yours for the modest price of a year's membership. It unlocks the treasures of 350 properties across the country, most of which are open every day during the summer. Special Events unfold all the pageantry and spectacle of the ages.

For further information ask at your Tourist Information Centre, or contact us direct at English Heritage, Membership Department, PO Box 1BB, London W1AA 1BB.

Then join us on a journey through time.

SEE WHERE GARDENS TELL A STORY

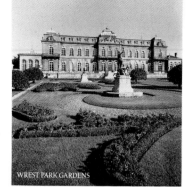

WREST PARK GARDENS

A CHAPEL CAME THROUGH FIRE

RYCOTE CHAPEL

AND A SKELETON CAME TO LIGHT

MINSTER LOVELL HALL

English ✛ Heritage

The National Trust

CLIVEDEN
Near Maidenhead

A magnificent garden high above the Thames with a Water Garden, Rose Garden, Parterre and garden sculpture. Once the home of Nancy, Lady Astor. Wonderful views over the river and miles of woodland walks. Present house built in 1851, now let to Blakeney Hotels Limited; three rooms open to visitors.

Refreshments in Orangery Restaurant; shop with wide selection of gifts. Free car park.

Cliveden is 2 miles north of Taplow on the B476 from the A5 (M4 junction 7 or M40 junction 4).
Tel: Burnham (06286) 5069.

OPEN: Grounds only: Mar to end Dec daily (inc. Good Fri) 11–6.
House: April to end Oct Thur and Sun 3–6 (by timed ticket).

STOWE LANDSCAPE GARDENS
Near Buckingham

Splendid landscape gardens with buildings and temples by Vanbrugh, Kent and Gibbs. One of the supreme creations of the Georgian era. (N.B. The main house is in the ownership of Stowe School.)

Stowe Landscape Gardens are 3 miles NW of Buckingham.

OPEN: During School Holidays, daily 10–6 (dusk if earlier). Last adm. 1 hour before closing. (School holidays: 1–10 Jan; 17 Mar–17 Apr; 7 July–4 Sept; 15–31 Dec; 1–8 Jan 1991) During Summer and Autumn terms: tel (0280) 822850 for details. Closed Good Fri, 25 and 26 Dec.

BASILDON PARK
Near Pangbourne

A fine Georgian house overlooking the Thames Valley, with important pictures, furniture and plasterwork. Attractive Octagon Room, and decorative Shell Room; garden and woodland walks.

Home-made teas in house; shop in stableyard. Free car park.

Basildon Park is 2½ miles NW of Pangbourne on the A329; 7 miles from M4 junction12.
Tel: Pangbourne (0734) 843040

OPEN: Apr to end Oct, Wed-Sat, 2–6; Sun and B. Hol Mons 1–6. Closed Good Fri and Wed after B.Hol. Last admission 5.30 p.m.

CLAYDON HOUSE
Near Buckingham

A fine 18th century house with fantastic rococo carvings in the state rooms. Florence Nightingale often visited Claydon and her bedroom and a museum with mementoes of her life and the Crimean War are on show.

Home-made teas available. Free car park.

Claydon is in Middle Claydon 13 miles NW of Aylesbury, signposted from A413, A421 and A41.
Tel: Steeple Claydon (029673) 349

OPEN: Apr to end Oct, Sat–Wed, 2–6; B.Hol Mons 1–6; Closed Good Fri. Last admission 5.30 p.m.

LUTON HOO
THE WERNHER COLLECTION

The works of Carl Fabergé, the Russian Court jeweller which are on view at Luton Hoo are part of the finest private collection of works of art in Great Britain which includes many continental treasures rarely seen in English Country Houses.

There are many paintings, costume and other personal possessions of the Russian Imperial Family Romanov, together with old masters by world famous artists, magnificent tapestries, English and French porcelain, Byzantine and medieval ivories, furniture, bronzes, statues and renaissance jewellery.

The park was landscaped by Capability Brown, and the rock gardens and formal gardens all contribute to making a visit well worthwhile.

OPEN DAILY 12 APRIL to 14 OCTOBER 1990 – 1.30pm to 5.45pm
CLOSED MONDAYS EXCEPT BANK HOLIDAYS

Admission £3.50 (Gardens only £1.50) S/Citizens £3.00 (£1.25) Children £1.50 (50p)

COACHES WELCOME – REFRESHMENTS – PICNIC AREA
FREE PARKING

Luton Hoo, Luton, Bedfordshire LU1 3TQ   Telephone (0582) 22955

Large variety of animals, birds and wildfowl.

Traditional farm shop.

Poultry and livestock centre, pure and rare breeds for sale.

Free picnic and play area.

Large car park.

Coffee shop.

Craft and gift shop.

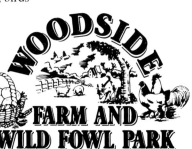

Opening hours:
Mon–Sat 8 am–
5.30pm, Sun Closed.

Wild Fowl Park:
Adults £1.00
OAP/Children 80p

Send large S.A.E. for brochure and price lists.

MANCROFT ROAD, SLIP END, LUTON, BEDS. Tel: Luton (0582) 841044

A Unique Victorian Natural History Collection

The Zoological Museum Tring, Hertfordshire

From dressed fleas to hairless dogs . . . unique memories of a by-gone age.

Through his passion for nature, Lionel, 2nd Baron Rothschild left an outstanding collection for all to see.

Museum shop sells a wide range of original gifts and natural history books.

How to get there: Akeman Street, Tring, Herts.
By road – Tring is on the A41, 7 miles SE of Aylesbury, 33 miles from London.
By public transport – Green Line hourly from Victoria.
London Country Buses. British Rail to Tring Station.

Open: Monday – Saturday 10.00 – 17.00
Sunday 14.00–17.00   Tel: Tring (044282) 4181

HATFIELD HOUSE

Celebrated Jacobean House (1611), Home of the Marquess of Salisbury
OPEN 25 MARCH TO 14 OCTOBER 1990

Every day except Mondays and Good Friday.
Also open on All Bank Holiday Mondays.
House Weekdays 12 noon–5pm, Sundays 1.30–5pm, Bank Holiday Mondays 11am–5pm.
Park 10.30am–8pm, Gardens 11am–6pm.

Large Park with Nature Trails and Adventure Play Area and Magnificent Gardens.
Garden and Gift Shops – Licensed Restaurant.
THE TONY DUROSE VEHICLE COLLECTION and THE NATIONAL COLLECTION OF MODEL SOLDIERS.

Living Crafts 1990–10 to 13 May.
Festival of Gardening 1990. 23 & 24 June.
National Patchwork Championships 1990–5 to 8 July.

For further details write or telephone:
The Curator, Hatfield House, Hertfordshire, AL9 5NQ. Telephone (0707) 262823.
Telex 265279 OLDPAL G

127

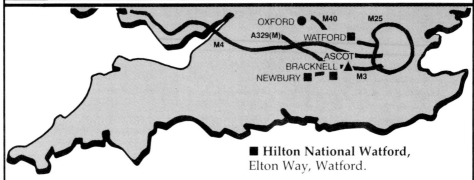

129

DIDCOT RAILWAY CENTRE

Recreating the golden age of the Great Western Railway. See steam engines in the original engine shed, a recreated station, Brunel's broad gauge and much more.

Open Saturdays and Sundays all year round and on Tuesdays to Sundays (and Bank Holiday Mondays) 1st April to 30th September. Steam trains run on the first & last Sunday of each month from March; Bank Holidays, all Sundays June-August and all Wednesdays in August.

Entrance at Didcot Parkway rail station (London Paddington 40 mins, Oxford 10 mins). On A4130 signed from A34 (M4 junction 13).

Spring Gala Steam Week 26 May–3 June

GREAT WESTERN SOCIETY: DIDCOT: OXFORDSHIRE   Tel: Didcot (0235) 817200

LEIGHTON BUZZARD RAILWAY

Take a ride on 'England's Friendly Little Line'

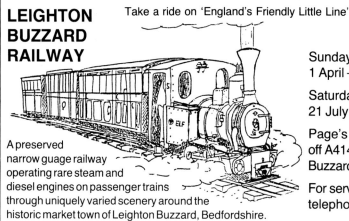

A preserved narrow guage railway operating rare steam and diesel engines on passenger trains through uniquely varied scenery around the historic market town of Leighton Buzzard, Bedfordshire.

OPEN

Sundays & BH Mondays
1 April – 7 October

Saturdays & Wednesdays
21 July – 29 August

Page's Park Station off A4146, Leighton Buzzard

For service & event details telephone: (0525) 373888

LOOKING FOR SOMEWHERE DIFFERENT TO TAKE THE FAMILY? LOOK NO FURTHER!

The age of steam lives on at Buckinghamshire Railway Centre where you can see giant express engines, small tank engines and ride in historic coaches

★ BUFFET ★
  ★ GIFT SHOP ★
    ★ MUSEUM ★
      ★ MINIATURE RAILWAY ★

Just seven miles north of Aylesbury. Follow the signs of A41 and A413 - lots of free parking

OPEN: Saturdays & Sundays · Easter to Oct.
also **Wednesdays to Fridays · June to Aug.**
Engines in steam on Wednesdays, Sundays and Bank Holiday Mondays.
Static displays on other days.

Quainton Road Station Nr. Aylesbury Bucks.

130

131

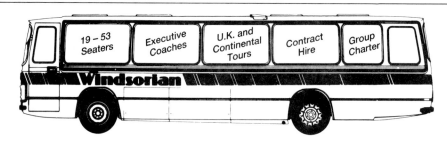

Enjoy a ·B·R·E·A·K·
The Spread Eagle Hotel
THAME ~ OXFORDSHIRE
for reservations telephone Thame (084 421) 3661

The Belfry Hotel

★ ★ ★
Milton Common
Oxford OX9 2JW
Telephone: 0884 279381
Fax: 0844 279624 Telex: 837968

60 bedrooms all with private facilities, colour TV, radio, telephone, tea/coffee facilities. LEISURE COMPLEX opening late 1989. Parking 200 cars. Extensive conference facilities. 40 minutes Heathrow. Situated on A40 near junction 7 of M40. Weekend Breaks.

The Priory Hotel

A beautifully preserved Tudor Courthouse AD1360, 5 miles north of Aylesbury. All 11 bedrooms, most with four-poster beds, are well appointed with private facilities. 'La Boiserie' restaurant is famous for its fine French cuisine, in a traditional and romantic English setting.

WHITCHURCH, AYLESBURY,
BUCKINGHAMSHIRE.
Telephone:
Aylesbury (0296) 641239

135

The Fox of Ibstone Country Hotel

👑 👑 👑 👑

near Henley-on-Thames
(1 mile off M40 at Junction 5)

This 300-year-old country inn is situated on the Chiltern Ridgeway, opposite Ibstone Common with its surrounding woodlands. Nine luxury double bedrooms with en-suite facilities, all have direct-dial telephone, hair dryer, trouser press, colour TV, radio, tea and coffee making facilities.
The attractive restaurant has an extensive à la carte menu. There are two bars with low beams, where real ale and a good cellar selection are served.
In the winter you will find open hearth log fires in both bars and restaurant.
Special Weekend Rates.

Ibstone, Nr High Wycombe, Bucks, HP14 3GG Telephone: (049-163) 289 and 722

A Warm Welcome Awaits

AT THE

WAYFARER

BAR & RESTAURANT

at Milton Keynes

Situated close to the heart of the metropolis and enjoying an idyllic setting overlooking Willen Lake. The Wayfarer offers 41 modern bedrooms with many facilities. Visit Kingfisher's Restaurant or take a drink on the Sundeck. The bar is open to all.

at Bedford

Strategically located on the A428 opposite Goldington Green and close to Elms Farm and Vikings Business Estate, The Wayfarer offers 29 bedrooms all with many features. Visit The Garden Room Conservatory Restaurant for à la carte cuisine. The bar is open to all.

PERFECT FOR EVERY OCCASION

The Wayfarer Hotel
Brickhill Street Willen Lake
Milton Keynes
Tel: (0908) 675222

The Wayfarer Hotel
Goldington Road
Goldington Bedford
Tel: (0234) 272707

The Coach and Horses

CHISLEHAMPTON
OXFORD OX9 7UX
TEL: (0865) 890255

A picturesque beamed XVth century inn & restaurant with nine modern individually heated bedrooms situated in rural Oxfordshire on B480 7 miles from Oxford City Centre and 5½ miles from Exit 7 M40. Table D'Hote, extensive à la carte menus and vegetarian dishes always available.

THE WALTON GUEST HOUSE

169 Walton Street, Oxford OX1 2HD
Tel. (0865) 52137

Situated in the city centre, this family run business is close to the University. For those wishing to travel further afield, the bus and railway stations are a mere five minutes walk away. For home comfort all rooms are fitted with central heating and each has colour television, tea and coffee making facilities. Throughout the year a full English Breakfast is served in the dining room. This accommodation is not suitable for the disabled. Sorry, no pets.

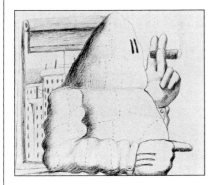

141

THE TRAVEL CLUB

your passport to the hidden charm of the Thames and Chilterns.

Polo in Windsor Great Park.

Join the Travel Club and you will see the five lovely counties of the Thames and Chilterns with the experts, not the tourists. This region contains some fine and fascinating sights, many of which the average tourist never gets to see.

Whatever your taste, the aim of the Travel Club is to help you make the most of everything that the Thames and Chilterns has to offer. For a subscription of just £10 per person a year (over half of which you receive back in the form of maps and other publications), you will be sent a monthly newsletter inviting you to a range of events in the coming month.

Membership of the Travel Club also entitles you to discounts at some hotels, restaurants, gardens and historic houses in the region. To join now please write to:

Stella Waterman,
The Travel Club,
Thames and Chilterns Tourist Board,
The Mount House,
Church Green,
Witney,
Oxon OX8 6DZ.

Index

143

145

Published by:
The Thames and Chilterns Tourist Board,
The Mount House,
Church Green,
Witney,
Oxon OX8 6DZ.
Tel. Witney (0993) 778800
Fax (0993) 779152
Telex 83343 ABTELX G.

Illustrations supplied by the establishments featured and: English Heritage, National Trust, Earl Beesley, John Bethell, British Tourist Authority, Ian Meredith, John Shore and Marilyn Yurdan.

Cartography by Estate Publications Ltd.

Typesetting and artwork by Opus, Oxford.

Printed by Bath Midway Press Ltd, Wiltshire.